PRINCE2™ Revealed

PRINCE2™ Revealed

including how to use PRINCE2™ for small projects

Colin Bentley

AMSTERDAM • BOSTON • HEIDELBERG • LONDON
NEW YORK • OXFORD • PARIS • SAN DIEGO
SAN FRANCISCO • SINGAPORE • SYDNEY • TOKYO

Butterworth-Heinemann is an imprint of Elsevier

Butterworth-Heinemann is an imprint of Elsevier
Linacre House, Jordan Hill, Oxford OX2 8DP, UK
30 Corporate Drive, Suite 400, Burlington, MA 01803, USA

First edition 2006
Reprinted 2006, 2007 (twice)

British Library Cataloguing in Publication Data
A catalogue record for this book is available from the British Library

Library of Congress Cataloging-in-Publication Data
A catalog record for this book is available from the Library of Congress

ISBN : 978-0-7506-6672-5

For information on all Butterworth-Heinemann publications
visit our website at books.elsevier.com

Printed and bound in *Great Britain*

07 08 09 10 10 9 8 7 6 5 4

Working together to grow
libraries in developing countries

www.elsevier.com | www.bookaid.org | www.sabre.org

ELSEVIER   BOOK AID International   Sabre Foundation

Contents

Contents

Preface

The method

'Project management is just common sense.' Of course it is. So why do so many of us get it wrong? Even if we get one project right, we probably make a mess of the next. And why do we keep getting it wrong time after time? You need to be armed with a little more than common sense when diving into a project such as constructing a pyramid. It is no good getting halfway through and then remembering you forgot to put in the damp course!

Why do so many professionals say they are project managing, when what they are actually doing is fire fighting?

The answer is that, where project management is concerned, most of us do not learn from our mistakes. We do not think about the process, document it, structure it, repeat it and use experience to improve the model. Problems are likely to arise in every project we tackle, but planning ahead and controlling how things happen against that plan could have avoided many of the problems the firefighter tackles.

Those who are starting a project for the first time should not have to reinvent the wheel. They should be able to build on the experience of previous project managers. By the time we are doing our tenth project we should have a method that helps us avoid mistakes we made in the previous nine.

This book presents PRINCE2™, a structured project management method based on the experience of scores of other project managers who have contributed, some from their mistakes or omissions, others from their success. It can be applied to any kind of project, however big or small; the basic philosophy is always the same. The method should be tailored to suit the size, importance and environment of the project. Common sense PRINCE2 says do not use a sledgehammer to crack a walnut but, equally, do not agree important things informally where there is any chance of a disagreement later over what was agreed.

These experiences show us why a good project management method such as PRINCE2 is needed if our projects are to be well managed and controlled.

PRINCE2 Revealed

- Statement 1 – Technical books are boring.
- Statement 2 – Technical books on PRINCE2 are very boring.
- Statement 3 – You may read a sentence in the manual and believe that you understand it, but when you come to do it in real life, the sentence only touched the tip of the iceberg and you are struggling.

I was reading a Dilbert book on holiday when the above thoughts struck me. Then another thought struck me (I was pretty badly damaged by now, with all these thoughts striking me); you may not be able to write about a project management method as if it were an exciting adventure story ('Two of the project assurance goons edged closer. "We'd like to talk to you about your last highlight report" one of them hissed, his beady eyes fastening on mine.'), or a classical romantic novel ('Her finger traced the outline of the work package in my hand. "I just love your quality criteria", she breathed, but her eyes held a different message'), but does it have to be as dry as dust?

I have put together some drawings of the events and words that I have heard about project management over the past quarter of a century or more, and I have added some thoughts on what lies hidden beneath some of the words in the PRINCE2 manual. I hope you find some humour in the drawings and some use in the experiences and thoughts that accompany them.

PRINCE2 for small projects

Why do so many project managers not use a project management method when managing small projects? But, first, what is 'a small project'?

When the author was with BP International's information technology (IT) department, a small project was anything costing less than £10 000 – and that was in the 1980s, so I would suggest that 'small' depends on the size of the company and the size of its 'normal' projects.

There are many projects that we can all identify as small, such as someone doing a house extension, the creation of an access database, the writing of a book, a supermarket reorganizing its displays, moving an office down the corridor, even the decoration of a hall and staircase. Most of these are tackled without the aid of a recognized project management method.

So how does your local builder carry out a successful project? Mostly it is based on years of experience. Usually behind this statement for any successful project manager lies a series of earlier projects where mistakes were made, such as materials or equipment not there when required, work tackled in the wrong sequence, requirements not fully understood at the outset, uncontrolled changes to requirements, customer dissatisfaction with the end result, and so on.

So, if all these pitfalls lie in wait for even the smallest project, why the reluctance to use a project management method? The answers given are usually 'they're too bureaucratic, top heavy', 'they are too expensive an overhead' and 'I haven't time' or 'my boss said "just do it"'.

This book tries to show that a project management method can be used on small projects without being costly in terms of money or time. In fact, it can save time and money, and deliver a better product.

Introduction

This book is based on the PRINCE2™ project management method. The method is owned by the Office of Government Commerce (OGC), an agency of the British government, and has been put in the public domain, so there is no fee to be paid for its use. (If you want to make money from the method, e.g. by offering training, products or consultancy, you need to get approval from OGC or the APM Group, contactable through Richard.pharro@apmgroup.co.uk)

The readers of this book will fall into three groups: those who have no prior knowledge of PRINCE2, those who know the theory of PRINCE2 and are interested in 'looking behind the scenes', and those who already know PRINCE2 and want to know how to apply it to small projects. The book is therefore divided into three physical parts: Part I to explain PRINCE2 to those new to it, Part II to dig under the surface of the method and get more insight into how to use it, and Part III to concentrate on the management of small projects. If you are new to PRINCE2, the suggestion is to read about it first. If you already know the method, dive straight into Part II of the book.

Layout of the book

Part I is an overview of PRINCE2 for those readers who are not yet well versed in the method. It covers the whole method, not in huge detail, but is enough to make the method understandable and to form the basis of using Parts II and III of the book.

Part II is a humorous (but useful) look at some aspects of PRINCE2 with guidance and templates on many bits that the official manual skims over.

Part III has six chapters, all tackling different approaches to scaling PRINCE2 for smaller projects.

Benefits of the PRINCE2 project management method

Organizations are becoming increasingly aware of the opportunities for adopting a 'project' approach to the way in which they address the creation and delivery of new business products or implement any change. They are also increasingly aware of the benefits which a single, common, structured approach to project management – as provided through PRINCE2 – can bring.

PRINCE2 is a scalable, flexible project management method, derived from the experience of professional project managers and refined over years of use in a wide variety of contexts. It is owned by a stable public authority, the Central Computing and Telecommunications Agency (CCTA), now part of the OGC. The CCTA has an ongoing commitment to maintaining the currency of the method and the tools that go with it, together with the information, books and manuals used to define the method.

- The method is repeatable.
- The method is teachable.
- It builds on experience.
- It insists that there should be a viable business case for a project before it begins and continues.
- It focuses on quality throughout the project life cycle.
- Everyone knows what to expect.
- If you take over a project in the middle, you know what documents to look for and where to find them.
- There is early warning of problems.
- It is proactive not reactive (but has to be prepared to be reactive to events – illness, pregnancy, accident, external events).

Finance

Use of the method is free. There is no purchase price and no annual licence fee for users.

Support

- The owners of the method, the OGC, have made a commitment to support its continuing evolution.
- The method was and is developed and enhanced by practising, professional project managers.
- There is a strong user group (in the UK, the Netherlands, Germany and Australia at present).
- PRINCE2 can be used for all types and sizes of project, encouraging its spread throughout organizations. For example, Tesco stores in Europe use it for all projects, including new store construction.
- The method is supported by over twenty specialist books.
- There is increasing software tool support for the method. Current tools are the PRINCEWorld Planning from Quality Projects International (an excellent product-based planning tool and lots more), and PRINCESS from WS Atkins. Navigo is being developed in the Netherlands, Tanner James in Australia have a good support tool, and TDL in UK have a powerful Internet and intranet tool called Project Architect for PRINCE2.
- There are regular examinations for project managers and also for project support personnel and those on the periphery of projects, such as auditors and quality assurance.
- The Foundation and Practitioner examination certificates, issued on behalf of OGC, are recognized worldwide.
- Over 100 000 candidates have taken the Practitioner examination in the UK so far. There are thousands more who have taken the examinations in the Netherlands, Australia and the USA.
- One or two UK companies have included PRINCE2 certification in their project management career path.
- Many UK project management advertisements in the national press ask for PRINCE2 knowledge or certification.

International spread

- The method and examinations are recognized and used in UK, the Netherlands, Denmark, Scandinavia, Poland, Hungary, Switzerland, Australia, North and South America, Hong Kong, Singapore, Italy, Bulgaria, China and Indonesia.
- The method has public and private sector users.
- Books on the method are available in Dutch, German, French, Italian and Spanish.

Quality control

- In order for any firm to be able to offer training or consultancy in the method to other organizations, the APM Group has first to formally accredit it. This accreditation has three parts:

  - The company has to show that it has the procedures and administrative capacity to provide and support courses.
  - The training material and course timetable are checked against the method and the syllabus.
  - Each trainer in the method must have passed both Foundation and Practitioner examinations, and scored well in the Practitioner examination. The trainer must have a curriculum vitae (CV) that shows solid project management experience. Each trainer is observed by the APM Group representative actually giving one or more sessions, and is then quizzed on their understanding of the method in general.

- All course delegates are asked to complete a feedback form, which is sent to the APM Group. A check is kept for any quality problems that may be voiced. If any arise, these are taken up with the management of the training organization.
- Every trainer is subject to continuous accreditation. Where a trainer cannot provide evidence of regular presentation experience in the method, he or she may be asked to go through the initial accreditation process again.
- Examination setting and marking is done by the APM Group, completely independent of the training organizations.
- Representatives of the APM Group may make ad hoc visits to any PRINCE2 course.
- When the manual has been revised, each training organization's material is reviewed, and training organizations are given advance warning of the manual changes to allow them to time the introduction of the new material with the publication of the revised manual.

Publicity

The APM Group has two well-established web sites, www.prince2.org.uk and www.apmgroup.co.uk.

- These contain details of all accredited training organizations and consultants, as well as a bookshop and a list of all those who have passed the examinations. A future web site will carry in-depth articles on the method to encourage regular visits by users.

- Magazine articles are regularly written for UK project management magazines.

Introduction

There are two key principles of PRINCE2™ that you should grasp as the basis for your understanding of the method:

- A project should be driven by its business case. You should not start a project unless there is a sound business case for it. At regular intervals in the project you check to see that the project is still viable and stop the project if the justification has disappeared.
- PRINCE2 is product based. PRINCE2 focuses on the products to be produced by the project, not the processes to produce them. This affects its method of planning, many of its controls and its approach to ensuring quality.

Structure of the PRINCE2 method

There are three parts to the structure of the method itself:

- processes
- components
- techniques.

PRINCE2 offers a set of processes that provide a controlled start, controlled progress and a controlled close to any project. The processes explain what should happen and when it should be done.

PRINCE2 has a number of components to explain its philosophy about various project aspects, why they are needed and how they can be used. This philosophy is implemented through the processes.

PRINCE2 offers only a few techniques. The use of most of them is optional. You may already have a technique that is satisfactorily covering that need. The exception is the product-based planning technique. This is a very important part of the PRINCE2 method. Its understanding and use bring major benefits and every effort should be made to use it.

Components

Figure 1 shows the components positioned around the central process model.

The components of PRINCE2 are:

- *Business case*: PRINCE2 emphasizes that a viable business case should drive a project. Its existence should be proved before the project is given the go-ahead and it should be confirmed at all major decision points during the project. Claimed benefits should be defined in measurable terms, so that they can be checked after delivery of the product.
- *Organization*: a structure of a project management team. A definition of the roles, responsibilities and relationships of

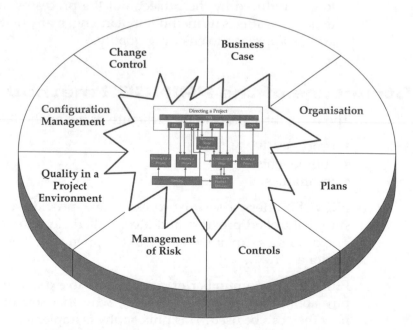

Figure 1 PRINCE2 Components

all staff involved in the project. PRINCE2 describes roles. According to the size and complexity of a project, these roles can be combined or shared.

- *Plans*: PRINCE2 offers a series of plan levels that can be tailored to the size and needs of a project, and an approach to planning based on products rather than activities.
- *Controls*: a set of controls which facilitate the provision of key decision-making information, allowing the organization to pre-empt problems and make decisions on problem resolution. For senior management PRINCE2 controls are based on the concept of 'management by exception', i.e. if we agree a plan, let the manager get on with it unless something is forecast to go wrong.
- A project is split into stages as an approach to defining the review and commitment points of a project in order to promote sound management control of risk and investment.
- *Management of risk*: risk is a major factor to be considered during the life of a project. PRINCE2 defines the key moments when risks should be reviewed, outlines an approach to the analysis and management of risk, and tracks these through all the processes.
- *Quality in a project environment*: PRINCE2 recognizes the importance of quality and incorporates a quality approach to the management and technical processes. It begins by establishing the customer's quality expectations and follows these up by laying down standards and quality inspection methods to be used, and checking that these are being used.
- *Configuration management*: tracking the components of a final product and their versions for release is called configuration management. There are many methods of configuration management available. PRINCE2 does not attempt to invent a new one, but defines the essential facilities and information requirements for a configuration management method and how it should link with other PRINCE2 components and techniques.
- *Change control*: PRINCE2 emphasizes the need for change control and this is enforced with a change control technique plus identification of the processes that apply the change control.

The processes

The steps of project management are described in eight processes, which are summarized in Figure 2.

3

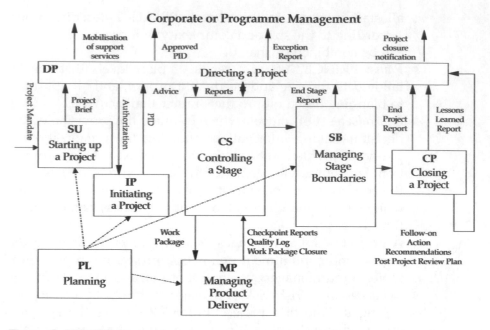

Figure 2 PRINCE2 Processes

A summary of the processes follows. Any project run under PRINCE2 will need to address each of these processes *in some form*. However, the key to successful use of the process model is in tailoring it to the needs of the individual project. Each process should be approached with the question 'How extensively should this process be applied on this project?'

Directing a project (DP)

This process is aimed at the senior management team responsible for the project – the key decision-makers. They are usually very busy people and should be involved only in the decision-making process of a project. PRINCE2 helps them achieve this by adopting the principle of 'management by exception'. The DP process covers the steps to be taken by this senior management team (the project board) throughout the project from start-up to project closure and has five major steps:

- authorizing the preparation of a project plan and business case for the project
- approving the project go-ahead

- checking that the project remains justifiable at key points in the project life cycle
- monitoring progress and giving advice as required
- ensuring that the project comes to a controlled close.

Starting up a project (SU)

This is intended to be a very short pre-project process with five objectives:

- ensuring that the aims of the project are known
- designing and appointing the project management team
- deciding on the approach which will be taken within the project to do the work
- agreeing the customer's quality expectations
- planning the work needed to draw up the PRINCE2 'contract' between customer and supplier.

Initiating a project (IP)

This process prepares the information on whether there is sufficient justification to proceed with the project, establishes a sound management basis for the project and creates a detailed plan for as much of the project as management are in a position to authorize. The management product created is the project initiation document, the baseline against which progress and success will be measured.

Controlling a stage (CS)

This process describes the monitoring and control activities of the project manager involved in ensuring that a stage stays on course and reacts to unexpected events. The process forms the core of the project manager's effort on the project, being the process that handles day-to-day management of the project development activity.

Throughout a stage there will be many cycles of:

- authorizing work to be done
- gathering progress information about that work
- watching for changes

- reviewing the situation
- reporting
- taking any necessary action.

The process covers these activities, together with the ongoing work of risk management and change control.

Managing product delivery (MP)

This process provides a control mechanism so that the project manager and specialist teams can agree details of the work required. This is particularly important where one or more teams are from third party suppliers not using PRINCE2. The work agreed between the project manager and the team manager, including target dates, quality and reporting requirements, is called a work package.

The process covers:

- making sure that work allocated to the team is authorized and agreed
- planning the teamwork
- ensuring that the work is done
- ensuring that products meet the agreed quality criteria
- reporting on progress and quality to the project manager
- obtaining acceptance of the finished products.

Managing stage boundaries (SB)

The objectives of this process are to:

- plan the next stage
- update the project plan
- update the business case
- update the risk assessment
- report on the outcome and performance of the stage which has just ended
- obtain project board approval to move into the next stage.

If the project board requests the project manager to produce an exception plan (see 'Controls' for an explanation), this process also covers the steps needed for that.

Closing a project (CP)

The process covers the project manager's work to request project board permission to close the project either at its natural end or at a premature close decided by the project board. The objectives are to:

- note the extent to which the objectives set out at the start of the project have been met
- confirm the customer's satisfaction with the products
- confirm that maintenance and support arrangements are in place (where appropriate)
- make any recommendations for follow-on actions
- ensure that all lessons learned during the project are annotated for the benefit of future projects
- report on whether the project management activity itself has been a success or not
- prepare a plan to check on achievement of the product's claimed benefits.

Planning (PL)

Planning is a repeatable process, used by the other processes whenever a plan is required. The process makes use of the PRINCE2 product-based planning technique and covers:

- designing the plan
- defining and analysing the plan's products
- identifying the necessary activities and dependencies
- estimating the effort required
- scheduling resources
- analysing the risks
- adding text to describe the plan, its assumptions and the quality steps.

Having gone through an introduction and overview of the method, Part I next focuses on the processes as the main theme. This will provide a project skeleton, a general project time frame. Where appropriate there will be links to the components and techniques, descriptions of which follow the processes.

Starting up a project (SU)

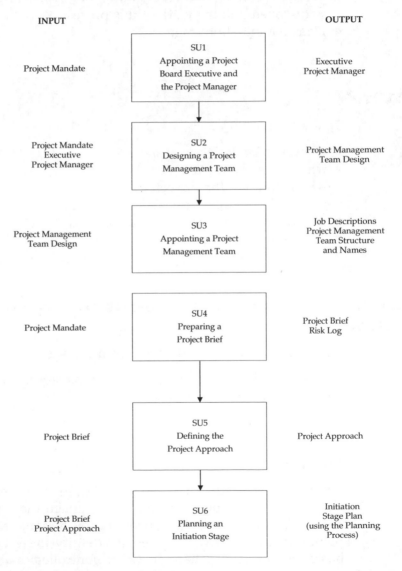

INPUT		OUTPUT
Project Mandate	**SU1** Appointing a Project Board Executive and the Project Manager	Executive Project Manager
Project Mandate Executive Project Manager	**SU2** Designing a Project Management Team	Project Management Team Design
Project Management Team Design	**SU3** Appointing a Project Management Team	Job Descriptions Project Management Team Structure and Names
Project Mandate	**SU4** Preparing a Project Brief	Project Brief Risk Log
Project Brief	**SU5** Defining the Project Approach	Project Approach
Project Brief Project Approach	**SU6** Planning an Initiation Stage	Initiation Stage Plan (using the Planning Process)

Figure 3 Top-level diagram (SU)

What does the process do?

- Completes (or confirms the existence of) terms of reference for the project.
- Appoints the project management team.
- Identifies the type of solution to be provided (the project approach).
- Identifies the customer's quality expectations.
- Creates a risk log and enters into it any risks known already or discovered in the work of this process.
- Plans the initiation stage.

Why?

To establish:

- what is to be done
- who will make the decisions
- who is funding the project
- who will say what is needed
- what quality standards will be required
- who will provide the resources to do the work.

SU1 – Appoint the executive and project manager

What does the sub-process do?

- Appoints the executive and project manager, prepares and signs their job descriptions.

Why?

Every project needs a sponsor, the key decision-maker. But normally this person is too busy to manage the project on a day-to-day basis. So we also need a project manager to do the planning and control. We need to identify these two people before anything can happen (in a controlled manner) in a project.

How?

- Corporate or programme management identify the executive to be responsible for the project.
- Either corporate/programme management or the executive, or both, identify a suitable project manager.
- The project manager starts with the standard PRINCE2 role descriptions for their jobs. These are then tailored by discussion between the executive and project manager.
- The tailored roles are typed up, both people sign two copies of their job descriptions. The individual keeps one; the other is kept by the project manager for filing once the project filing system has been set up.

SU2 – Design the project management team

What does the sub-process do?

- Proposes the other project board members.
- Discusses with the project board members whether they will need help to carry out their assurance responsibilities.
- Designs any project assurance roles to be delegated.
- Identifies candidates for any project assurance roles to be delegated.
- Identifies any required team managers.
- Identifies any project support requirements.

Why?

The complete project management team needs to reflect the interests, and have the approval of:

- corporate/programme management
- the users of the final product, those who will specify details of the required product
- the supplier(s) of that product.

Project board members must decide whether they want independent checks on their particular interests in the project as the project progresses (the project assurance part of the role), or whether they can do this verification themselves.

The project manager has to decide if any administrative support is needed, such as planning and control tool expertise, configuration management, filing or help with specialist techniques.

How?

- Identify customer areas that will use or control the end product, the commitment required and the level of authority and decision-making which is suitable for the criticality and size of the project (senior user).
- Identify who will provide the end product(s) (supplier) and the level of commitment authority required from them.
- Identify candidates for the roles.
- Check out their availability and provisional agreement.
- Check whether the project board members will carry out their own project assurance responsibilities.
- Identify candidates for any project assurance functions which are to be delegated.
- Check out their availability.
- Decide if any project support will be required.
- Identify resources for any required support.

SU3 – Appoint the project management team

What does the sub-process do?

- The other project board members, any required project assurance and project support roles are appointed.
- There may also be team managers to be appointed, particularly for the early stages.

Why?

A job description for each member of the project management team needs to be agreed with the individual.

After the project management team has been designed, the appointments need to be confirmed by corporate/programme management.

How?

- The project management team design is presented to corporate/programme management for approval.
- The executive informs each project management team member of their appointment.
- The project manager discusses and agrees each member's job description with them.

SU4 – Preparing a project brief

What does the sub-process do?

- Fills in any gaps in the project mandate handed down.

Why?

To ensure that sufficient information is available for the project board to decide if it wishes to proceed into initiation.

How?

- Compare the information available about the required project against the information required by the project board in order to approve project initiation.
- Advise the project board how long it will take to prepare for the project initiation meeting.
- Gather any missing information such as:
  - objectives, deliverables, scope, constraints
  - customer's quality expectations.
- Check the business case with the executive.

SU5 – Defining project approach

What does the sub-process do?

- Decides on what kind of a solution (project approach) will be provided and the general method of providing that solution.
- Identifies the skills required by the project approach.
- Identifies any timing implications of the project approach.

- The main project approaches to be considered are:
  - build a solution from scratch
  - take an existing product and modify it
  - give the job to another organization to do for you
  - buy a ready-made solution off the shelf.

Why?

The project approach will affect the timescale and costs of the project, plus possibly its control over scope and quality. This information should be made available to the project board in deciding whether to initiate the project.

A check should be made that the proposed project approach is in line with the customer's (or programme) strategy.

How?

- Identify any time, money, resource, operational support or later product extension constraints.
- Check for any direction or guidance on project approach from earlier documents such as the project mandate.
- Identify any security constraints.
- Check for any corporate/programme statement of direction which might constrain the choice of project approaches.
- Consider how the product might be brought into use and whether there are any problems which would impact the choice of project approach.
- Produce a range of alternative project approaches.
- Identify the training needs of the alternatives.
- Compare the alternatives against the gathered information and constraints.
- Prepare a recommendation.

SU6 – Planning an initiation stage
What does the sub-process do?

- Produces a plan for the initiation stage of the project.

Why?

Investigating and establishing the foundation of a project, then preparing a document to get approval to start the project is important work. It needs planning and, since initiation will consume some resources, the project board should approve the plan for it.

How?

- Examine the project brief and decide how much work is needed in order to produce the project initiation document.
- Evaluate the time needed to create the project plan.
- Evaluate the time needed to create the next stage plan.
- Evaluate the time needed to create or refine the business case.
- Evaluate the time needed to perform risk analysis.
- Create a plan for the initiation stage.
- Get project board approval for the plan.

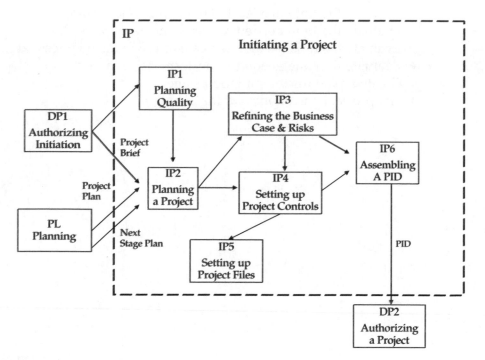

Figure 4 Top-level diagram (IP)

What does the process do?

- Defines the quality responsibilities and quality methods and tools to be used.
- Plans the whole project.
- Lays the foundation for a well-planned and controlled project.

- Expands and confirms the existence of a viable business case.
- Reassesses the risks facing the project.
- Gets all the decision-makers to sign up to the project.
- Prepares the next stage plan.

Why?

All stakeholders with interest in the project should reach agreement before major expenditure starts on what is to be done and why it is being done.

IP1 – Planning project quality

What does the sub-process do?

- Takes the quality expectations of the customer, the quality standards of both customer and supplier and the project approach and defines how the quality expected by the customer will be achieved.

Why?

To be successful, the project must deliver a quality product, as well as meeting time and cost constraints. The means of achieving quality must be specified before work begins.

Quality work cannot be planned until the quality expectations of the customer are known.

The time and cost of the project will be affected by the amount of quality work that has to be done; therefore, quality planning must be done before a realistic project plan can be produced.

How?

- Establish links to any corporate or programme quality assurance function.
- Establish what the customer's quality standards are.
- Establish what the supplier quality standards are.

17

- Decide if there is a need for an independent quality assurance function to have representation on the project management team.
- Identify quality responsibilities for project products of both the customer and supplier in their job descriptions.
- Establish how quality will be achieved.
- Create the quality log.
- Identify any required change control procedures and produce a configuration management plan.

IP2 – Planning a project

What does the sub-process do?

- Produces the project plan.

Why?

As part of its decision on whether to proceed with the project, the project board needs to know how much it will cost and how long it will take. Details of the project plan also feed into the business case to indicate the viability of the project.

How?

- Use the 'planning' process to create the project plan.
- Review the plan against any project constraints.
- Modify the plan accordingly.
- Decide on a suitable breakdown of the project into stages.
- Check that the plan meets the requirements of the project quality plan.
- Check the plan informally with the project board.

IP3 – Refining the business case and risks

What does the sub-process do?

- Takes whatever outline business case exists for the project, plus the project plan, and creates a full business case for inclusion in the project initiation document.
- Carries out a further risk analysis and management for the project based on the new information created.

Why?

Before commitment to the project it is important to ensure that there is sufficient justification for the resource expenditure and that there is a sound balance between business justification and the risks.

How?

- If a business case was included in the project mandate, check if its circumstances and assumptions have changed.
- Investigate the work reasons for the project with the customer.
- Investigate the business reasons for the project with the executive.
- Quantify the benefits wherever possible.
- Incorporate the costs from the project plan.
- Perform risk analysis.
- Modify the project plan to reflect any changes caused by risk analysis.

IP4 – Setting up project controls

What does the sub-process do?

- Establishes control points and reporting arrangements for the project, based on the project's size, criticality, risk situation, the customer's and supplier's control standards, and the diversity of stakeholders.

Why?

In order to keep the project under control it is important to ensure that:

- the right decisions are made by the right people at the right time
- the right information is given to the right people at the right frequency and timing.

How?

- Agree the stage breakdown with the project board.
- Agree the format of reports to the project board and stake-holders.

- Agree the frequency of project board and stakeholder reports.
- Establish reporting requirements from team(s) to the project manager.
- Check that there are sufficient risk and business case monitoring activities in the plans.

IP5 – Setting up project files

What does the sub-process do?

- Sets up the filing structure for management records for the project. Filing or storage needs for the specialist products will depend on the type of products being produced.

Why?

It is important to retain details of key events, decisions and agreements. These details may help in future project estimation, provide input to the lessons learned log and final report or provide a historical record of what happened, when and why. This is particularly important if relationships between customer and supplier turn sour because of, for example, disputes on scope or costs.

How?

- Create the issue log.
- Create project and stage files.
- Establish any configuration management method required by the configuration management plan (created in IP1).
- Set up a blank lessons learned log to record useful points throughout the project.

IP6 – Assembling a project initiation document (PID)

What does the sub-process do?

- Gathers together the information from the other IP sub-processes and assembles the project initiation document.
- Invokes the sub-process SB1 (planning a stage) to produce the next stage plan.

Why?

The project initiation document encapsulates all the information needed for the project board to make the decision on whether to go ahead with the project or not. It also forms a formal record of the information on which the decision was based, and can be used after the project finishes to judge how successful the project was.

If the project board makes a general decision to proceed with the project, it needs to have more detailed information about the costs and time of the next stage before committing the required resources.

How?

- Assemble the required information.
- Decide how best to present the information.
- Create the project initiation document.
- Invoke sub-process SB1 (planning a stage) to produce the next stage plan.
- Check that the plan meets the requirements of the project quality plan.
- Distribute the two documents to the project board, any others with project assurance roles, and any other stakeholders.

Directing a project (DP)

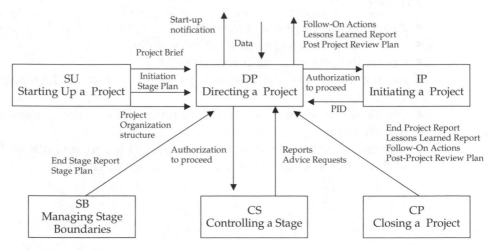

Figure 5 Top-level diagram (DP)

What does the process do?

- Authorizes project initiation.
- Provides liaison with corporate/programme management.
- Advises the project manager of any external business events which might impact the project.
- Approves stage plans.
- Approves stage closure.
- Decides on any changes to approved products.
- Approves any exception plans.

- Gives ad hoc advice and direction throughout the project.
- Safeguards the interests of the customer and supplier.
- Approves project closure.

Why?

Day-to-day management is left to the project manager, but the project board must exercise overall control and take the key decisions.

DP1 – Authorizing initiation

What does the sub-process do?

- Checks that adequate terms of reference exist.
- Checks and approves the initiation stage plan.
- Commits the resources required to carry out the initiation stage work.

Why?

The initiation stage confirms that a viable project exists and that everybody concerned agrees what is to be done. Like all project work, the effort to do this needs the approval of the project board.

How?

- Confirm the terms of reference, checking if necessary with corporate/programme management.
- Check the initiation stage plan and approve it if satisfied.
- Agree tolerance margins for the initiation stage.
- Agree control and reporting arrangements for the initiation stage.
- Commit the resources required by the plan.

DP2 – Authorizing a project

What does the sub-process do?

- Decides whether to proceed with the project or not.
- Approves the next stage plan.

Why?

The sub-process gives the project board a decision point before major resource commitment to the project.

How?

- Confirm that the project's objectives and scope are clearly defined and understood by all.
- Confirm that the objectives are in line with corporate/programme objectives.
- Confirm that all authorities and responsibilities are agreed.
- Confirm that the business case is adequate, clear and, wherever possible, measurable.
- Confirm the existence of a credible project plan which is within the project constraints.
- Check that the plan for the next stage is reasonable and matches that portion of the project plan.
- Have any desired changes made to the draft project initiation document.
- Confirm tolerance levels for the project and the next stage.
- Give written approval for the next stage (or not, if unhappy with any of the details).
- Arrange a date for the next stage's end stage assessment.

DP3 – Authorizing a stage or exception plan

What does the sub-process do?

- The sub-process authorizes each stage (except initiation) and any exception plans that are needed.

Why?

An important control for the project board is to approve only one stage at a time. At the end of one stage the project manager has to justify both progress so far and the plan for the next stage before being allowed to continue.

How?

- Compare the results of the current stage against the approved stage plan.
- Assess progress against the project plan.
- Assess the acceptability of the next stage plan against the project plan.
- Review the prospects of achieving the business case.
- Review the risks facing the project.
- Get direction from corporate/programme management if the project is forecast to exceed tolerances or there is a significant change to the business case.
- Review tolerances for the next stage.
- Review reporting arrangements for the next stage.
- Give approval to move into the next stage (if satisfied).

DP4 – Giving ad hoc direction

What does the sub-process do?

- Advises the project manager about any external events which impact the project.
- Gives direction to the project manager when asked for advice or a decision about a project issue.
- Advises on or approves any changes to the project management team.
- Makes decisions on the actions to take on receipt of any exception reports.

Why?

There may be a need for occasional and immediate project board direction outside end stage assessments.

How?

- Check for external events, such as business changes, which might affect the project's business case or risk exposure.
- Monitor any allocated risk situations.
- Make decisions on any exception reports.
- Ensure that the project remains focused on its objectives and achievement of its business case.

25

- Keep corporate/programme management and stakeholders advised of project progress.
- Make decisions about any necessary changes to the project management team.
- Make decisions on project issues brought to the attention of the project board.

DP5 – Confirming project closure

What does the sub-process do?

- Checks that the objectives of the project have been met.
- Checks that there are no loose ends.
- Advises senior management of the project's termination.
- Recommends a plan for checking on achievement of the expected benefits.

Why?

There must be a defined end to a project in order to judge its success. The project board must assure itself that the project's products have been handed over and are acceptable. Where contracts (and money) are involved, there must be agreement between customer and supplier that the work contracted has been completed.

How?

- The supplier gains acceptance from the customer that all the required products have been delivered and the acceptance criteria have been met.
- Check that there has been a satisfactory handover of the finished product(s) to those responsible for its use and support.
- Check that there are no outstanding project issues.
- Approve the follow-on action recommendations and pass them to the appropriate group.
- Approve the lessons learned report and pass it to the appropriate body.

- Approve the end project report.
- Release the resources allocated to the project.
- Advise corporate/programme management of the project's closure.
- The project board disbands the project management team.

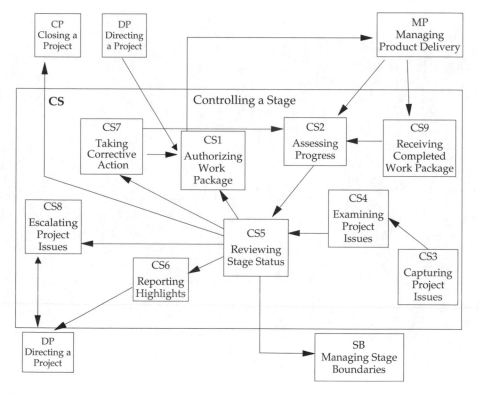

Figure 6 Top-level diagram (CS)

What does the process do?

- Manages the stage from stage approval to completion.

Why?

The production of the stage's products within budget and schedule and to the required quality must be driven by the project manager and also requires careful monitoring and control.

CS1 – Authorizing work package

What does the sub-process do?

- Allocates work to be done to a team or individual, based on the needs of the current stage plan.
- Ensures that any work handed out is accompanied by measurements such as target dates, quality expectations, delivery and reporting dates.
- Ensures that agreement has been reached on the reasonableness of the work demands with the recipient.

Why?

The project manager must control the sequence of at least the major activities of a stage and when they begin. This ensures that the project manager knows what those working on the project are doing, and that the stage plan correctly reflects the work and progress.

How?

- Ensure that there is a product description for the work to be done and that this is complete.
- Make up the work package.
- Discuss the work package with the team manager.
- Jointly assess any risks or problems and modify the work package and risk log as necessary.
- Ensure that sufficient resources and time have been allocated for the work.
- Record the agreement of the team manager in the work package.
- Update the stage plan with any adjustments made as part of the agreement.

CS2 – Assessing progress

What does the sub-process do?

- Gathers information to update the stage plan to reflect actual progress, effort expended and quality work carried out.

Why?

In order to control the stage and make sensible decisions on what, if any, adjustments need to be made, it is necessary to gather information on what has actually happened and be able to compare this against what was planned.

How?

- Collect checkpoint reports.
- Collect stage plan progress information (possibly in the form of timesheets).
- Obtain estimates on time, cost and effort needed to complete work which is in progress.
- Check whether sufficient resources are available to complete the work as now estimated.
- Check the feedback on quality activities.
- Update the stage plan with the information.
- Note any potential or real problems.

CS3 – Capturing project issues

What does the sub-process do?

- Captures, logs and categorizes new project issues.

Why?

At any time during the project a problem may occur, a change may be requested or the answer to a question may be sought. If these are missed, it may mean that the project fails to deliver what is required. Alternatively the project may run into some other trouble that could have been foreseen, had the issue been noted at the time it arose. There must be a process to capture these so that they can be presented for the appropriate decision and response.

How?

- The project manager ensures that all possible sources of issues are being monitored.
- New issues are entered on the issue log.

CS4 – Examining project issues

What does the sub-process do?

- Analyses each new project issue and recommend a course of action.
- Reviews each open project issue for any change to its circumstances or impact and potentially make a new recommendation.
- Reviews all open project issues for any impact on the project risks or the business case.

Why?

Having captured all issues in the sub-process 'Capturing project issues' (CS3), these should be examined for impact and the appropriate body for any extra information and decision identified.

How?

- Assemble all pertinent information about the project issue.
- Carry out impact analysis on the technical effort required to resolve the project issue.
- Update the risk log if the project issue reveals a new risk or a change to a known risk.
- Assess whether the project issue or its resolution would impact the business case.
- Prepare a recommended course of action.
- Update the issue log with the impact analysis result.

CS5 – Reviewing stage status

What does the sub-process do?

- Provides a regular reassessment of the status of the stage.
- Triggers new work.

- Triggers corrective action for any problems.
- Provides the information for progress reporting.

Why?

It is better to check the status of a stage on a regular basis and take action to avoid potential problems than have problems come as a surprise and then have to react to them.

How?

- Review progress against the stage plan.
- Review resource and money expenditure.
- Review the impact of any implemented project issues on stage and project plans.
- Assess if the stage and project will remain within tolerances.
- Check the continuing validity of the business case.
- Check for changes in the status of any risks.
- Check for any changes external to the project which may impact it.

CS6 – Reporting highlights

What does the sub-process do?

- Produces highlight reports for the project board.

Why?

The project board and stakeholders need to be kept informed of project progress if it is to exercise proper control over the project. Rather than have regular progress meetings, reports at regular intervals are recommended between assessments at the end of each stage. The project board decides the frequency of the reports at project initiation.

How?

- Collate the information from any checkpoint reports made since the last highlight report.
- Identify any significant stage plan revisions made since the last report.

- Identify any current or potential risks to the business case.
- Assess the issue log for any potential problems which require project board attention.
- Identify any change to other risks.
- Report a summary of this information to the project board.

CS7 – Taking corrective action

What does the sub-process do?

- Within the limits of the tolerance margins established by the project board, the project manager takes action to remedy any problems that arise.

Why?

Failing to take action when the project is drifting away from the stage plan invites loss of control.

How?

- Obtain any necessary advice from the project board on the proposed corrective actions.
- Create new work packages or amend existing ones to reflect the corrective actions.

CS8 – Escalating project issues

What does the sub-process do?

- Where an issue threatens to go beyond tolerances and the project manager feels that he/she cannot take corrective action within the authority limits imposed by the project board, the situation must be brought to the attention of the project board for advice.

Why?

Part of the concept of management by exception is that the project manager will bring to the immediate attention of the project board anything that can be forecast to drive the plan

33

beyond the tolerance limits agreed with the project board. This is part of the project board staying in overall control.

How?

- Carry out an impact analysis of the deviation.
- Identify and evaluate options for recovery.
- Select a recommendation.
- Make out an exception report to the project board, detailing the problem.

CS9 – Receive completed work package

What does the sub-process do?

- This sub-process records the completion and return of approved work packages.

Why?

Where work has been recorded as approved to a team or individual, there should be a matching sub-process to record the return of the completed product(s) and its/their acceptance (or otherwise).

How?

- Check the delivery against the requirements of the work package.
- Obtain quality confirmation.
- Check that the recipients have accepted the products.
- Ensure that the delivered products have been baselined.
- Document any relevant team member appraisal information.
- Pass information about completion to update the stage plan.

Managing product delivery (MP)

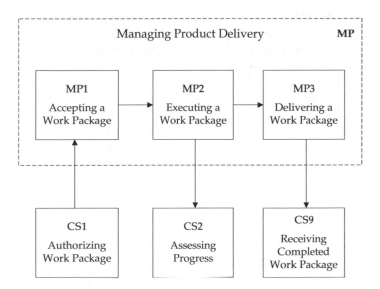

Managing Product Delivery   **MP**

MP1	MP2	MP3
Accepting a Work Package	Executing a Work Package	Delivering a Work Package

CS1	CS2	CS9
Authorizing Work Package	Assessing Progress	Receiving Completed Work Package

Figure 7 Top-level diagram (MP)

What does the process do?

- Agrees work requirements with the project manager.
- Does the work.
- Keeps the project manager informed on progress, quality and any problems.
- Gets approval for the finished work.
- Notifies the project manager that the work is finished.

Why?

Where the project manager delegates work, there must be appropriate steps by the team or person to whom the work is delegated to indicate understanding and acceptance of the work. While the work is being done, there may be a need to report progress and confirm quality checking. When the work is complete there should be an agreed way of confirming the satisfactory completion.

MP1 – Accepting a work package

What does the sub-process do?

- Agrees the details of a work package with the project manager.
- Plans the work necessary to complete the work package.

Why?

There must be understanding and agreement between a team manager (or an individual) and the project manager on any delegated work.

How?

- Agree with the project manager on what is to be delivered.
- Ensure that the quality requirements are clear.
- Identify any independent people who must be involved in quality checking.
- Identify any target dates and/or constraints for the work.
- Identify any reporting requirements.
- Understand how the products of the work package are to be handed over when complete.
- Make a plan to do the work.
- Perform the management of risk against the work package plan.
- Check the plan against the work package.
- Adjust the plan or negotiate a change to the work package so that the work package is achievable.
- Agree suitable tolerance margins for the work package.

MP2 – Executing a work package

What does the sub-process do?

- Manages the development/supply of the products/services defined in the work package.

Why?

Having agreed and committed to work in MP1, this sub-process covers the management of that work until its completion.

How?

- Allocate work to team members.
- Capture and record the effort expended.
- Monitor progress against the tolerances agreed for the work.
- Monitor and control the risks.
- Evaluate progress and the amount of effort still required to complete the product(s) of the work package.
- Feed progress reports back to the project manager at the frequency agreed in the work package.
- Ensure that the required quality checks are carried out.
- Ensure that any personnel identified in the work package are involved in the quality checking.
- Update the quality log with results of all quality checks.
- Raise project issues to advise the project manager of any problems.

MP3 – Delivering a work package

What does the sub-process do?

- Obtains approval of the products developed/supplied.
- Hands over the products to whoever is responsible for configuration management.
- Advises the project manager of the completion of the work.

Why?

There has to be a sub-process to deliver the requested product(s) and document the agreement that the work has been done satisfactorily.

How?

- Confirm that the quality log has been updated with details of a successful check on the quality of the product(s).
- Obtain approval from whoever is defined in the work package as the end user of the product(s).
- Transfer the products and control of their release to the project's configuration librarian.
- Advise the project manager that the work package is complete.
- Where necessary, obtain a documented appraisal from the project manager of the performance in completing the work package.

Managing stage boundaries (SB)

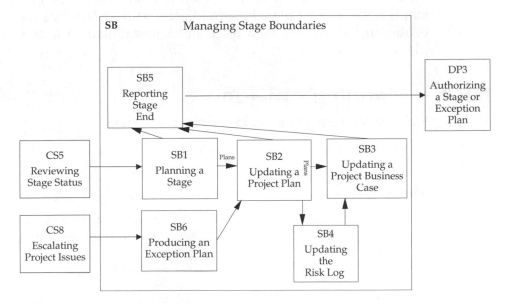

Figure 8 Top-level diagram (SB)

What does the process do?

- Confirms to the project board which products planned to be produced in the current stage plan have been delivered.
- Gives reasons for the non-delivery of any products which were planned (in the case of deviation forecasts).
- Verifies that any useful lessons learned during the current stage have been recorded in the lessons learned log.
- Provides information to the project board to allow it to assess the continued viability of the project.

39

- Obtains approval for the next stage plan or the exception plan.
- Ascertains the tolerance margins to be applied to the new plan.

Why?

The ability to authorize a project to move forward a stage at a time is a major control for the project board. There is also a need for a process to create a plan to react to a forecast deviation beyond tolerances. This process aims to provide the information needed by the project board about the current status of the project plan, business case and risks to judge the continuing worth of the project and commitment to a new plan.

SB1 – Planning a stage

What does the sub-process do?

- Prepares a plan for the next stage.

Why?

In order to adequately control a stage the project manager needs a plan in which the detailed activities go down to the level of a handful of days.

How?

- Check the project approach for any guidance on how the products of the next stage are to be produced.
- Check the issue log for any issues which will affect the next stage plan.
- Use the common planning (PL) process to create the draft plan.
- Document any changes to the personnel of the project management team.
- Discuss the draft plan with those who have project assurance responsibilities.
- Add any formal quality reviews and any other quality checks required for project assurance purposes.

- Identify (as a minimum) the chairperson of each formal quality review.
- Identify with those with project assurance responsibilities the required reviewer skills and authority required for each formal quality review.
- Ensure that the plan includes all required management products.
- Check the plan for any new or changed risks and update the risk log.
- Modify the plan, if necessary, in the light of the risk analysis.

SB2 – Updating a project plan

What does the sub-process do?

- The project plan is updated with the actual costs and schedule from the stage that has just finished, plus the estimated cost and schedule of the next stage plan.

Why?

As one stage is completed and the next one planned, the project plan must be updated so that the project board has the most up-to-date information on likely project costs and schedule on which to partially base its decision on whether the project is still a viable business proposition.

How?

- Ensure that the current stage plan has been updated with final costs and dates.
- Create a new version of the project plan ready to be updated.
- Update the new version of the project plan with the actual costs and dates of the current stage.
- Update the project plan with the estimated costs, resource requirements and dates of the next stage.
- Update any later stages of the project plan on the basis of any relevant information made available since the last update.
- Check to see if events mean that the project approach has to be modified.

41

SB3 – Updating a project business case

What does the sub-process do?

- Modifies the business case, where appropriate, on the basis of information from the current stage and the plan for the next stage.

Why?

The whole project should be business driven, so the project board should review a revised business case as a major part of the check on the continued viability of the project.

How?

- Create a new version of the business case ready to be updated.
- Review the expected costs in the investment appraisal against the new forecast in the updated project plan.
- Review the financial benefits in the investment appraisal against any new forecasts.
- Review the reasons in the business case and check that there has been no change or that no new reasons have come to light.
- Modify the new version of the business case in the light of any changes to forecast.

SB4 – Updating the risk log

What does the sub-process do?

- Checks the known risks to project success for any change to their circumstances and looks for any new risks.

Why?

Part of the assessment of the project's viability is an examination of the likelihood and impact of potential risks.

How?

- Ensure that the risk log is up-to-date with the latest information on the identified risks.
- Ensure that any new risks identified in creating the next stage plan have been entered on the risk log.
- Assess all open risks to the project, as defined in the risk log.
- Decide if the next stage plan needs to be modified to avoid, reduce or monitor risks.
- Create contingency plans for any serious risks which cannot be avoided or reduced to manageable proportions.

SB5 – Reporting stage end

What does the sub-process do?

- Reports on the results of the current stage.
- Forecasts the time and resource requirements of the next stage, if applicable.

Why?

Normally the project board manages by exception and therefore only needs to meet if things are forecast to deviate beyond tolerance levels. But as part of its control the project board only gives approval to the project manager to undertake one stage at a time, at the end of which it reviews the anticipated benefits, costs, timescale and risks and makes a decision whether to continue with the project or not.

How?

- Report on the actual costs and time of the current stage and measure these against the plan which was approved by the project board.
- Report on the impact of the current stage's costs and time taken on the project plan.
- Report on any impact from the current stage's results on the business case.
- Report on the status of the issue log.
- Report on the extent and results of the quality work done in the current stage.

43

- Provide details of the next stage plan (if applicable).
- Identify any necessary revisions to the project plan caused by the next stage plan.
- Identify any changes to the business case caused by the next stage plan.
- Report on the risk situation.
- Recommend the next action (e.g. Approval of the next stage plan).

SB6 – Producing an exception plan

What does the sub-process do?

- In response to an exception report the project board may request the project manager to prepare a new plan to replace the remainder of the current plan.

Why?

The project board approves a stage plan on the understanding that it stays within its defined tolerance margins. When an exception report indicates that the current tolerances are likely to be exceeded, the project board may ask for a new plan to reflect the changed situation and which can be controlled within newly specified tolerance margins. The project board may take other measures, such as premature closure of the project or removal of the problem causing the deviation.

How?

- An exception plan has exactly the same format as a stage plan.
- An exception plan covers the time from the present moment to the end of the plan that is to be replaced.

Closing a project (CP)

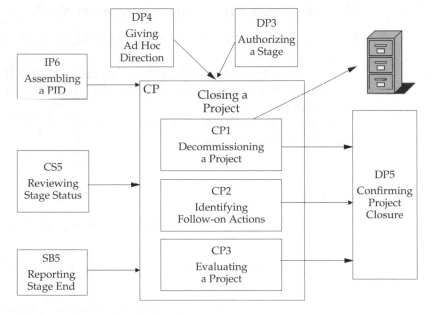

Figure 9 Top-level diagram (CP)

What does the process do?

- Checks that all required products have been delivered and accepted.
- Checks that all project issues have been dealt with.
- Records any recommendations for subsequent work on the product.
- Passes on any useful lessons learned during the project.
- Recommends closure of the project to the project board.
- Plans to measure the achievement of the project's business case.

Why?

Every project should come to a controlled completion.

In order to have its success measured, a project must be brought to a close when the project manager believes that it has met the objectives set out in the project contract.

CP1 – Decommissioning the project

What does the sub-process do?

- Gets agreement from the customer that the acceptance criteria have been met.
- Confirms acceptance of the project's product from the customer and those who will support the product during its operational life.
- Checks that all project issues are closed.
- Arranges archiving for the project files.

Why?

The customer and supplier must agree that a project has met its objectives before it can close.

There must be a check that there are no outstanding problems or requests.

The project documentation, particularly agreements and approvals, should be preserved for any later audits.

How?

- Check that all project issues have been closed.
- Get the customer's agreement that the acceptance criteria have been met.
- Ensure that all products have been completed and accepted by the customer.
- Ensure that, where applicable, those who will be responsible for maintenance and support of the products are ready to accept the product.
- Complete and archive the project files.

CP2 – Identifying follow-on actions

What does the sub-process do?

- Identifies any work which should be done following the project.
- Prepares a plan for when the realization of the project's expected benefits should be checked.

Why?

Any knowledge of unfinished business at the end of a project should be documented, checked with the project board and passed to the appropriate body for action.

How?

- Check for any omissions in the product or suggestions on how to improve the product and put these on the follow-on action recommendations.
- Ensure that the omissions and suggestions are recorded as follow-on action recommendations.
- Check the issue log for any issues which were not completed or rejected and transfer them to the follow-on action recommendations.
- Check the risk log for any risks that may affect the product in its operational life and add these to the follow-on action recommendations.
- Identify when measurement can be made that the product has delivered its benefits and prepare a plan to carry out that measurement.

CP3 – Project evaluation review

What does the sub-process do?

- Assesses the project's results against its objectives.
- Provides statistics on the performance of the project.
- Records useful lessons that were learned.

Why?

One way in which to improve the quality of project management is to learn from the lessons of past projects.

As part of closing the project, the project board needs to assess the performance of the project and the project manager. This may also form part of the customer's appraisal of a supplier, to see if the contract has been completed, or to see if that supplier should be used again.

How?

- Write the end project report, evaluating the management, quality and technical methods, tools and processes used.
- Complete the lessons learned report from the following.
- Examine the risk log and actions taken, and record any useful comments.
- Examine the issue log and actions taken, and record any useful comments.
- Examine the quality log and record any useful comments.

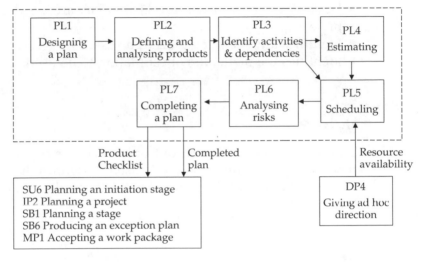

Figure 10 Top-level diagram (PL)

What does the process do?

- Defines the levels of plan needed for the project.
- Decides what planning tools and estimating methods will be used.
- Identifies the products whose delivery has to be planned.
- Identifies the activities needed to deliver those products and the dependencies between them.
- Estimates the effort needed for each activity.
- Allocates the activities to resources and schedules the activities against a time frame.
- Analyses the risks inherent in the plan.
- Adds explanatory text to the final plan.

Why?

PRINCE2 offers a standard way in which to produce any level of plan. This means that all plans will have the same format and method of development. The process is based around the PRINCE2 technique of product-based planning.

PL1 – Designing a plan

What does the sub-process do?

- Decides on how many levels of plan are needed by the project.
- Identifies any planning tools to be used.
- Identifies the method(s) of estimating to be used.

Why?

This sub-process is carried out only once per project, the first time that the planning process is used. It defines the standards to be used in all future plans. The result should be a consistent set of plans.

How?

- Decide on what levels of plan are needed for the project, i.e. project plan, stage plans, team plans.
- Ascertain if the organization or programme uses a particular planning tool as standard.
- Identify the planning tool to be used in the initial project plan, part of the project initiation document.
- Identify what estimating method(s) are available and suitable for the project.
- Ensure that the estimating method(s) chosen contain allowances for project issue, analysis, telephone calls, ad hoc meetings, learning curves, experience, etc.
- Discuss with the project board whether there should be a change budget set aside.
- Discuss with the project board whether there should be a separate allowance for any anticipated contingency plans.

PL2 – Defining and analysing products

What does the sub-process do?

- Identifies the products whose delivery has to be planned.
- Describes each of the products in terms of purpose, composition and quality criteria, and ensures that these descriptions are agreed by all concerned.
- Identifies the sequence of delivering the products and the dependencies between them.

Why?

By defining the products and their quality requirements everyone can see and understand the required plan result. It means that whoever has to deliver a product knows in advance what its purpose is, to what quality it has to be built and what interfaces there are with other products.

How?

- Identify the products required.
- Write product descriptions for them.
- Draw a diagram showing the sequence of delivery and dependencies between the products.
- Optionally produce a product checklist.

PL3 – Identifying activities and dependencies

What does the sub-process do?

- Identifies all activities necessary to deliver the products.
- Defines the dependencies between the activities.

Why?

For stage and team plans the product flow diagram (PFD – created in sub-process PL2) may still be at too high a level for the purposes of estimation and control. This optional sub-process allows a further breakdown, based on the PFD until each activity will last only a handful of days.

How?

- Consider if a product in the PFD is too big to estimate or would need such a large effort that it would be difficult to control against that estimate.
- Where a product is too big, break it down into the activities needed to produce it. This should continue down to the level where an activity is less than ten days' effort, and ideally no more than five days'.
- Where a product has been broken down into several activities, put the activities into their correct sequence.
- Review the dependencies between products and refine them to give dependencies between the new activities. For example, where PFD dependencies went from the end of one product to the start of the next, is there now an opportunity to overlap, or to start some activities on a product before all the activities on its preceding product have been done?

PL4 – Estimating

What does the sub-process do?

- Identifies the types of resource needed for the plan.
- Estimates the effort for each activity/product.

Why?

The objective is to identify the resources and effort required to complete each activity or product.

How?

- Examine each activity/product and identify what resource types it requires. Apart from human resources there may be other resources needed, such as equipment. With human resources, consider and document what level of skill you are basing the estimate on.
- Judge what level of efficiency you will base your estimates on, what allowance for non-project time you will need to use.
- Estimate the effort needed for each activity/product.

- Understand whether that is an estimate of uninterrupted work, to which the allowances must be added, or whether the estimate already includes allowances.
- Document any assumptions you have made, e.g. the use of specific named resources, levels of skill and experience, the availability of user resources when you need them.
- Check the assumptions with those who have such knowledge, such as the senior supplier and senior user.

PL5 – Scheduling

What does the sub-process do?

- Matches resources to activities/products.
- Schedules work according to sequence and dependencies.
- Adjusts the schedule to avoid people being over- or under-used.
- Negotiates a solution with the Project Board for problems such as too few resources, too many resources or inability to meet fixed target dates.
- Calculates the cost of the resources used in the plan.

Why?

A plan can only show whether it can meet its targets when the activities are put together in a schedule against a time frame, showing when activities will be done and by what resources.

How?

- Draw a planning network.
- Assess resource availability. This should include dates of availability as well as what the scale of that availability is. Any known information on holidays and training courses should be gathered.
- Allocate activities to resources and produce a draft schedule.
- Revise the draft to remove as many peaks and troughs in resource usage as possible.
- Add in management and quality activities or products (stage and team plans only).
- Calculate resource utilization and costs.

PL6 – Analysing risks

What does the sub-process do?

- Checks the draft plan for any risks in it.

Why?

You should not commit to a plan without considering what risks are involved in it and what impact the plan might have on risks already known.

How?

- Look for any external dependencies. These always represent one or more risks. They might not arrive on time. They might be of poor quality or be wrong in some other way.
- Look for any assumptions you have made in the plan, e.g. the resources available to you. Each assumption is a risk.
- Look at each resource in the plan. Is there a risk involved? For example, that a new resource does not perform at the expected level, or a resource's availability is not achieved.
- Are the tools or technology unproven?
- Take the appropriate risk actions. Where appropriate, revise the plan. Make sure that any new or modified risks are shown in the risk log.

PL7 – Completing a plan

What does the sub-process do?

- Adds text to explain the plan.

Why?

A plan in diagrammatic form is not self-explanatory. It needs text.

How

- Agree tolerance levels for the plan.
- Document what the plan covers, the approach to the work and the checking of its quality.
- Document any assumptions you have made.
- Add the planning dates to the product checklist (if used).
- Publish the plan.

Philosophy

Every project should be driven by a business need. If it has no justification in terms of the business, it should not be undertaken.

The business case is a vital project management tool. It should be considered before any project is commissioned, ideally at a higher level such as the strategy group, and certainly as part of any feasibility study stage.

- The contents of a business case should include the reasons for the project, the prioritized business benefits, costs of the proposed solution, a cost/benefit analysis, a good, average and poor (GAP) analysis and a sensitivity analysis. The last two are explained in a little more detail later in the chapter.
- Well-constructed business cases will have assessed the impact of doing nothing and will identify the differences achieved by implementing the proposed solution.

A high-level business case should be included in the project mandate. If it is not, then one should be added as part of developing the project brief.

The business case should be formally reviewed at the start of a project, and again at stage boundaries and at project closure. It should also be reviewed when major change requests are made. It should be monitored continuously throughout the project.

If a project is part of a larger programme, its justification will point at the business case of the programme. In such a case, the project may have no business justification itself, but contribute to achievement of the programme business case. In this case, the reviews mentioned above will refer back to the continuing need for the project within the perceived needs for the programme.

Overview

The business case contains the following components.

Reasons

This is a narrative description of the justification for undertaking the project.

Benefits

A narrative description of what the expected benefits are, plus estimated benefit figures over the life of the product. Benefits should be defined in terms that are

- measurable at the start of the project
- measurable when the final product is in use.

Cost and timescale

The estimated development and running costs for the project and the expected delivery date.

Investment appraisal

This considers what would happen if the project was not done – none of the costs would be incurred and the benefits would not be accrued. This is known as the 'do nothing' option and is used as the benchmark against which the predicted costs and benefits are measured.

It is important to remember that the 'do nothing' option should be calculated by assessing the implications of staying with the current mode of operation for the anticipated life of the new product/service/system.

The 'do something' option

Estimates of the implications of implementing the project's solution need to be made in a similar way and over a similar time period to the 'do nothing' option above.

Project managers often make the mistake, when developing or refining the business case, of quantifying benefit and cost implications themselves. This is not usually wise. It is sensible to get the users to quantify benefits. They may need a little help from you, but the figures should be recognized as theirs. When the product's real benefits are finally measured, you do not want the user accusing you of overestimating its value.

Cash flow

The business case is calculated by establishing the difference between the 'do something' option and the 'do nothing' option and comparing this with the investment cost required for the project.

Links

As mentioned earlier, a basic business case should appear in the project mandate, or be developed as part of preparing a project brief (SU4).

There is a major link with the initiation stage, in which the project manager should finalize the business case before the project board decides whether the project should be undertaken.

The business case should be revised at the end of each stage in SB4, updating the business case. This feeds into the end stage assessment, which is the review by the project board in DP3, authorizing a stage or exception plan, as part of its decision on whether to continue with the project.

The impact on the business case is assessed for each major project issue as part of the sub-process CS4, examining project issues.

Achievement of the business case is finally judged in the post-project review.

The implications of risk management should be linked to the business case.

Do's and don'ts

Do examine the business case if those who will use the final product put it up. Be sure that the business case figures are genuine, not just pulled out of the air. Many impressive business cases are put up to endorse a political wish or whim, but do not stand up to close scrutiny.

If you are the supplier, beware of the temptation to write the customer's business case. The customer has to 'own' the business case. The customer may need some help in thinking in financial terms of how to justify the project, but if the project should run into cash trouble, you do not want the customer saying 'But you said it was justifiable'.

If it is a large project

The business case is likely to take some time to prepare. There should have been at least the outline of a business case in the project mandate that triggered the project.

If it is a small project

Do not ignore the philosophy that there should be business justification for every project. A lot of small projects undertaken without business justification can waste as much as one large project. It may be satisfactory to carry out a short, informal business case appraisal, but the executive should still be convinced that a genuine business case exists.

Project organization

Philosophy

The organization for any project should be based on a customer/ supplier relationship. The customer is the person or group who wants the end product, specifies what it should be and, usually, pays for the development of that product. The supplier is whoever provides the resources to build or procure the end product. This is true even if the customer and supplier work for the same company. If this is the case they may still, for example, report to different lines of management, have different budgets and, therefore, have a different view of the finances of the project. The customer will be asking, 'Will the end product save me money or bring in a profit?' The supplier will be asking if the providing of appropriate resources will earn a profit.

Establishing an effective organizational structure for the project is crucial to its success. Every project needs direction, management, control and communication. Before you start any project you should establish what the project organization is to be. You need to ask the questions *even if it is a very small project*. Answers to these questions will separate the real decision-makers from those who have opinions, identify responsibilities and accountability, and establish a structure for communication. Examples of the questions to ask are:

- Who is providing the funds?
- Who has the authority to say what is needed?
- Who is providing the development resources?
- Who will manage the project on a day-to-day basis?
- How many different sets of specialist skills are needed?
- Who will establish and maintain the required standards?

- Who will safeguard the developed products?
- Who will know where all the documents are?
- What are the limits to the Project Manager's authority and who sets those limits?

Overview

To fulfil the philosophy, I offer for your consideration a project management team structure (Figure 11).

It would be good if we could create a generic project management structure that could be tailored to any project. Without knowing anything about a project's size or complexity we could understand the same organizational terms and, by fitting names to these, understand quickly who does what. But if we were to have one structure for all sizes of project, it would be important that we made it flexible, a structure that would be adequate for large as well as small projects. The only way in which we can do this is to talk about *roles* that need to be filled, rather than jobs that need to be allocated on a one-to-one basis to individuals. In order to be flexible and meet the needs of different environments and different project sizes, our structure will define roles that might be allocated to one person, shared with others or combined according to a project's needs. Examples are given later in the chapter.

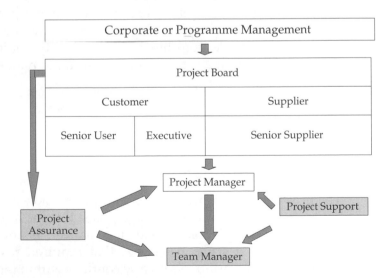

Figure 11 A project management team structure

Corporate or programme management hand the decision-making for a project to the project board. The project board members are busy in their own right and do not have the time to look after the project on a day-to-day basis. They delegate this to the project managers, reserving to themselves the key stop/go decisions. If they are too busy or do not have the current expertise, they can appoint someone to a project assurance role to monitor an aspect of the project on their behalf. A typical example here would be the participation of a company's quality assurance function on behalf of the senior user or the senior supplier. (Note: they would take a project assurance role as far as PRINCE2 is concerned, not quality assurance – QA.) Another example of the project assurance role would be a role for internal audit.

Depending on the project environment or the project manager's expertise, he or she might need some support. This might be purely administration, such jobs as filing or note-taking, but it also includes specialist jobs such as configuration management or expertise in the planning and control software tool that is to be used on the project.

Project board

General

The project board is appointed by corporate/programme management to provide overall direction and management of the project. The project board is accountable for the success of the project, and has responsibility and authority for the project within the limits set by corporate/programme management.

The project board is the project's 'voice' to the outside world and is responsible for any publicity or other dissemination of information about the project.

Specific responsibilities

The project board approves all major plans and authorizes any major deviation from agreed stage plans. It is the authority that signs off the completion of each stage as well as authorizes the start of the next stage. It ensures that required resources are committed and it arbitrates on any conflicts within the project or negotiates a solution to any problems between the project and external bodies. In addition, it approves the appointment and responsibilities of the project manager and any delegation of its project assurance responsibilities.

The project board is ultimately responsible for project assurance, i.e. that it remains on course to deliver the desired outcome of the required quality to meet the business case defined in the project contract. According to the size, complexity and risk of the project, the project board may decide to delegate some of this project assurance responsibility. Later in this chapter project assurance is defined in more detail.

Responsibilities of specific members of the project board are described in the respective sections below.

Executive

General

The executive is ultimately responsible for the project, supported by the senior user and senior supplier. The executive has to ensure that the project is value for money, ensuring a cost-conscious approach to the project, balancing the demands of business, user and supplier.

Throughout the project the executive 'owns' the business case.

The executive is responsible for overall business assurance of the project, i.e. that it remains on target to deliver products that will achieve the expected business benefits, and the project will complete within its agreed tolerances for budget and schedule.

Senior user

General

The senior user is responsible for the specification of the needs of all those who will use the final product(s), user liaison with the project team and for monitoring that the solution will meet those needs within the constraints of the business case.

The role represents the interests of all those who will use the final product(s) of the project, those for whom the product will achieve an objective, or those who will use the product to deliver benefits. The senior user role commits any required user resources and monitors products against requirements. This role may require more than one person to cover all the user interests. For the sake of effectiveness the role should not be split between too many people.

Senior supplier

General

Represents the interests of those designing, developing, facilitating, procuring, implementing, operating and maintaining the project products. The senior supplier is responsible for the quality of all products supplied by the suppliers. The role must have the authority to commit or acquire supplier resources required.

If necessary, more than one person may be required to represent the suppliers.

Project manager

General

The project manager has the authority to run the project on a day-to-day basis on behalf of the project board within the constraints laid down by the board. In a customer/supplier environment the project manager will normally come from the customer organization.

The project manager's prime responsibility is to ensure that the project produces the required products, to the required standard of quality and within the specified constraints of time and cost. The project manager is also responsible for the project producing a result that is capable of achieving the benefits defined in the business case.

Team manager

General

The allocation of this role to one or more people is optional. Where the project does not warrant the use of a team manager, the project manager takes the role.

The project manager may find that it is beneficial to delegate the authority and responsibility for planning the creation of certain products and managing a team of technicians to produce those products. There are many reasons why it may be decided to employ this role. Some of these are the size of the project, the particular specialist skills or knowledge needed for certain products, the geographical location of some team members and the preferences of the project board.

The team manager's prime responsibility is to ensure production of those products defined by the project manager to an appropriate quality, in a timescale and at a cost acceptable to the project board. The team manager reports to and takes direction from the project manager.

The use of this role should be discussed by the project manager with the project board and, if the role is required, planned at the outset of the project. This is discussed later in the starting up a project (SU) and initiating a project (IP) processes.

Project assurance

General

The project board members do not work full-time on the project; therefore they place a great deal of reliance on the project manager. Although they receive regular reports from the project manager, there may always be questions at the back of their minds, e.g. 'Are things really going as well as we are being told?' 'Are any problems being hidden from us?' 'Is the solution going to be what we want?' 'Are we suddenly going to find that the project is over-budget or late?' There are other questions. The supplier may have a quality assurance function charged with the responsibility to check that all projects are adhering to the quality system.

All these points mean that there is a need in the project organization for independent monitoring of all aspects of the project's performance and products. This is the project assurance function.

To cater for a small project, we start by identifying these project assurance functions as part of the role of each project board member. According to the needs and desires of the project board, any of these project assurance responsibilities can be delegated, as long as the recipients are independent of the project manager and the rest of the project management team. Any appointed project assurance jobs assure the project on behalf of one or more members of the project board.

It is not mandatory that all project assurance roles be delegated. Each project assurance role that is delegated may be assigned to one individual or shared. The project board decides when a project assurance role needs to be delegated. It may be for the entire project or only part of it. The person or persons filling a project assurance role may be changed during the project at the request of the project board. Any use of project assurance roles needs to be planned at initiation stage, otherwise resource usage and costs for project assurance could easily get out of control.

There is no stipulation on how many project assurance roles there must be. Each project board role has project assurance responsibilities. Again, each project should determine what support, if any, each project board role needs to achieve this assurance. For example, an international standards group, such as the International Standards Organization (ISO) may certificate the supplier's work standards. A requirement of the certification is that there will be some form of quality assurance function that is required to monitor the supplier's work. Some of the senior supplier's project assurance responsibilities may be delegated to this function. Note that they would only be delegated. The project board member retains accountability. Any delegation should be documented. The quality assurance could include verification by an external party that the project board is performing its functions correctly.

Project assurance covers all interests of a project, including all business, user and supplier.

Project assurance has to be independent of the project manager; therefore the project board cannot delegate any of its project assurance responsibilities to the project manager.

Project support

General

The provision of any project support on a formal basis is optional. It is driven by the needs of the individual project and project manager. Project support could be in the form of advice on project management tools and administrative services, such as filing or the collection of actual data, to one or more related projects. Where set up as an official body, project support can act as a repository for lessons learned, and a central source of expertise in specialist support tools.

One support function that must be considered is that of configuration management. Depending on the project size and environment, there may be a need to formalize this, and it quickly becomes a task with which the project manager cannot cope without support. See the chapter on configuration management for details of the work.

Plans

Overview

This chapter looks at the question of planning for a project. Figure 12 introduces a suggested hierarchy of plans.

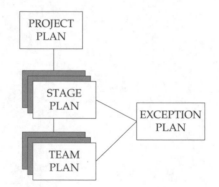

Figure 12 Hierarchy of plans

Project plan

The project plan is created at the start of the project. The initial project plan is a part of the project initiation document. The project plan is a mandatory plan.

The project board does not want to know about every detailed activity in the project. It requires a high-level view. This allows the project board to know:

- how long the project will take
- what the major deliverables or products will be
- roughly when these will be delivered

- what people and other resources will have to be committed in order to meet the plan
- how control will be exerted
- how quality will be maintained
- what risks are there in the approach taken.

The project board will control the project using the project plan as a yardstick of progress.

Stage plan

Stage plans are mandatory. Unless a project is very small it will be easier to plan in detail one stage at a time. Another part of the philosophy that makes stage planning easier is that a stage is planned shortly before it is due to start, so you have the latest information on actual progress so far available to you.

Having specified the stages and major products in the project plan, each stage is then planned in a greater level of detail. This is done, as previously mentioned, just before the end of the previous stage.

The procedure at stage planning time involves taking those major products in the project plan that are to be created during that stage, and breaking these down (typically) to a further two or three levels of detail.

Plan narrative

The project and stage plans should have a narrative section. Suggested headings for the narrative are as follows:

- Plan description
- Quality plan
- Plan assumptions
- Plan prerequisites
- External dependencies
- Risks
- Tolerance
- Reporting.

69

Team plan

Team plans are optional. Their use or otherwise is dictated by the size, complexity and risks associated with the project.

Team plans are the lowest level of detail and specify activities down to the level of a handful of days, say ten at most. Team plans may or may not contain the narrative sections associated with the higher levels.

Team plans will be needed when internal or external teams are to do portions of the work. Part of the project manager's job is to cross-relate these plans to the project and stage plans.

Exception plan

Finally, there is the exception plan. This is produced when a plan is predicted to exceed the time and cost agreed between the planner and the next higher level of authority. If a team plan is forecast to deviate beyond tolerances, the team manager must produce the exception plan and get approval for its introduction from the project manager. If a stage plan is forecast to deviate, the project manager will produce an exception plan and ask the project board to allow the exception plan to replace the current stage plan. If the project plan threatens to go beyond its tolerances, the project board must take the exception plan to corporate or programme management.

The exception plan takes over from the plan it is replacing and has the same format.

Project controls

Introduction

Project control is perhaps the key element in project management. Some would say that risk management is the cornerstone of project management, but, although I deal with risk management in its own chapter, I see it as one part of control. Whatever your opinion, I think we can all agree it is vital. I have divided 'control' into the various areas shown in Figure 13.

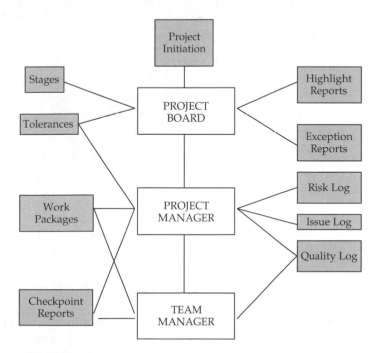

Figure 13 Control areas

Project initiation

However large or small the project, it is sensible to begin a project with what is referred to in PRINCE2 as project initiation. This is where the project board and project manager decide if there is agreement on:

- what the project is to achieve
- why it is being undertaken
- who is to be involved and in what role
- how and when the required products will be delivered.

This information is documented in the project initiation document, which is then 'frozen' and used by the project board as a benchmark throughout the project, and at the end to check the performance and deliveries of the project.

Stages

A stage is a collection of activities and deliverables whose delivery is managed as a unit. As such, it is a subset of the project, and in PRINCE2 terms it is the element of work that the project manager is managing on behalf of the project board at any one time.

Stage-limited commitment: at the end of each stage the project board only approves a detailed plan to produce the products of the next stage. The project plan is updated, but this is mainly for the guidance of the project board and will become more accurate as more stages are completed.

The reasons for breaking projects into management stages are to give the project board opportunities for conscious decision-making as to whether to continue with the project or not, based upon:

- a formal analysis of how the project is performing, based on information about results of the current stage
- an assessment of the next stage plan
- a check on what impact the next stage plan will have on the overall project plan
- a check to confirm that the business justification for the project and product is still valid confirmation that the risks facing the project are manageable.

In theory, at the end of each stage, the project board can call for cancellation of the project because of the existence of one or more possibly critical situations. For example, the organization's business needs may have changed to the point at which the project is no longer cost-effective. A project may also be cancelled if the estimated cost to complete it exceeds the available funds. In practice, however, cancellation of a project becomes progressively more difficult to justify as increasing amounts of resources are invested.

Unless the project is broken into stages to provide suitable points at which to make the decisions, the project board cannot be fully in control of the project and its resources.

Tolerance

Tolerance is the permissible deviation from a plan without having to refer the matter to the next higher level of authority.

No project has ever gone 100 per cent to plan. There will be good days and bad days, good weeks and bad weeks. If the project board is going to 'manage by exception' it does not want the project manager running to it, saying, 'I've spent a dollar more than I should today' or 'I've fallen half a day behind schedule this week'. But, equally, the project board does not want the project to overspend by £1 million or slip two months behind schedule without being warned. So where is the dividing line? What size of deviation from the plan is OK without going back to the board for a decision? These margins are the tolerances.

The second philosophical point about tolerances is that we do not wait for tolerances to be exceeded; we forecast this, so that the next higher level of authority has time to react and possibly prevent or reduce the deviation or exception.

The two main elements of tolerance are time and cost. Other elements to be considered are scope, quality benefit and risk.

- Corporate/programme management sets the project tolerances within which the project board has to remain.
- The project board agrees stage tolerances with the project manager.
- The project manager agrees tolerances for a work package with a team manager.

73

As long as the plan's actual progress is within the tolerance margins, all is well. As soon as it can be *forecast* that progress will deviate outside the tolerance margins, the next higher level of authority needs to be advised.

Project tolerances should be part of the project mandate handed down by corporate/programme management. If they are not there, it is the executive's job to find out from corporate/programme management where they are.

The project board sets stage tolerances for the project manager within the overall project tolerances that they have received. The portion allocated to a stage should depend on the risk content of the work, the extent of the unknowns such as technologies never used before, resources of unknown ability and tasks never attempted before.

The project manager negotiates appropriate tolerances for each work package with the team manager. Again these will be sub-tolerances within the stage tolerances set for the project manager.

End stage assessments

The end stage assessment occurs at the end of each management stage, where the project board assesses the continued viability of the project and, if satisfied, gives the project manager approval to proceed with the next stage.

The project board must be aware of the need to avoid technical or irrelevant discussions and to focus on the management aspects which, when taken as a whole, inform its decision on whether to proceed or not. As a rule of thumb an end stage assessment should not last more than two hours. A sensible project manager will have been in touch with the project board, either verbally or in highlight reports, making sure that the members know what is coming and finding out what they think about the future of the project. 'No surprises' is the best way to ensure short end stage assessments.

Of course, the 'bottom line' is whether the project is still predicted to deliver sufficient benefits to justify the investment, i.e. is the business case still sound?

Highlight reports

The best way of characterizing *management by exception* is the expression 'no news is good news'. At a frequency defined by the project board in the project initiation document, the project manager has to send a highlight report to the project board to confirm progress and achievements in the current stage.

The frequency of highlight reports is determined by the project board during initiation, but is typically produced monthly.

The project manager prepares highlight reports, using progress information provided by the team members and analysed at the checkpoints.

Risk log

Risks are examined:

- before starting the project
- before commencing a new stage
- as part of the analysis of any major change
- before confirming project closure.

Project issues

Having approved the objectives and products required in the project initiation, it is only right that the project board should have to approve any changes to them. Once the effort and cost of requested changes have been estimated, the customer has to decide on their priority, whether they should be done and whether the money to do them can be found. As for all the other decisions, these need an assessment of the impact on the project plan, the business case and the risk situation.

Exception reports

If the project manager can forecast that the plan will end outside its tolerance margins, an exception report must be sent immediately to the project board, detailing the problem, options and a recommendation.

Work packages

A work package is an agreement between the project manager and either an individual or a team manager to undertake a piece of work. It describes the work, agreed dates, standards to be used, quality and reporting requirements. No work can start without the project manager's approval via a work package, so it is a powerful schedule, cost and quality control for the project manager.

Checkpoint reports

This is a report from a team manager to the project manager. It is sent at a frequency agreed in the work package.

A specific aim of a checkpoint report is to check all aspects of the work package against the team and stage plans to ensure that there are no hidden nasty surprises. Useful questions to answer are: 'What is not going to plan?' and 'What is likely not to go to plan?' The crucial question that underlies the objective of the meeting is 'Are we still likely to complete the stage within the tolerances laid down by the project manager?' The information gathered in checkpoint reports is recorded for the project manager and forms the basis of the highlight report.

Quality log

The quality log records every planned quality check, plus details of when it actually happened, who participated and what the results were. It provides the project manager with an overview of what is happening with regard to quality. Either team managers or team members add details of the actual quality events.

Philosophy

Any thoughts or actions about quality in a project must start by finding out what the customer's quality expectations are. It is dangerous to assume that the customer will always want a superb quality product that will last for ever. Have a look at the products in your local cut-price store and you will see what I mean.

The quality path

Table 1 Quality path.

Step	Product	Process/technique
Ascertain the customer's quality expectations	Project mandate or project brief	Starting up a project (SU)
Write a project quality plan	Project initiation document	Initiating a project
Write a stage quality plan	Stage plan	Managing stage boundaries
Define a product's quality criteria	Product descriptions	Product-based planning
Explain the quality requirements for each piece of work	Work package	Controlling a stage
Report back on the quality work performed	Quality log	Managing product delivery
Check that quality work is being done correctly	Quality log	Controlling a stage
Control changes	Project issue	Change control
Keep track of changes to products	Configuration item records	Configuration management

Customer's quality expectations

The customer's quality expectations should be made clear in the project mandate at the very outset of the project. If not sufficiently clear, the project manager should clarify the expectations when preparing the project brief (during starting up a project – SU). The expectations should be measurable. 'Of good quality' may sound fine, but how can it be measured? Expectations of performance, reliability, flexibility, maintainability, and capability can all be expressed in measurable terms.

The project quality plan

The next step is to decide how the project is going to meet the customer's quality expectations for the product. Other inputs to this should be the standards to be used to guide the development of the product and test its ability to meet the quality expectations. The supplier should have standards, but the customer may also have standards that it insists on being used. Such standards have to be compared against the expectations to see which are to be used. There may be gaps where extra standards have to be obtained or created. The customer has the last say in what standards will be used to check the products. There may also be regulatory standards to be met.

The project quality plan identifies the standards to be used and the main quality responsibilities. The latter may be a reference to a quality assurance function (belonging to the customer, the supplier, or both). There is a cross-reference here to the project board roles. These roles contain project assurance responsibilities, some of them affecting quality. If these have been delegated, there must be a match with the responsibilities defined in the project quality plan.

The project quality plan refers to the establishment of the quality log, the quality file and their purposes. The plan also identifies the procedures that will be used to control changes and the configuration management plan.

Product descriptions are written for the key products shown in the project plan. These include specific quality criteria against which the products will be measured.

The stage quality plan

Each stage has its own quality plan containing lower-level detail than the project quality plan. This identifies the method of quality checking to be used for each product of the stage. The plan also identifies responsibilities for each individual quality check. For example, for each quality review the chairperson and reviewers are identified. This gives an opportunity for those with project assurance roles to see each draft stage plan and input its needs for checking and the staff who should represent it at each check.

Any major products developed in the stage have product descriptions written for them, if they were not done as part of the project quality plan.

Product descriptions

A product description should be written for each major product to be produced by the project.

The product description should be written as soon as possible after the need for it is recognized. Writing the description helps the planner understand what the product is and how long it is likely to take to build it.

The product description is also the first place where we start thinking about the quality of the product, how we will test the presence of its quality and who we might need in order to test that quality.

It is very sensible to get the customer to write as much of the product description as possible, particularly its purpose and quality criteria. This helps the customer define what is needed and is useful when delivering a product to be able to confirm that a product meets its criteria.

The product description is an important part of the information handed to a team manager or individual as part of a work package.

Any time that a product that has been approved by the project board has to be changed, the product description should also be checked to see if it needs an update.

Quality file

The project manager should keep a file of all the quality checking information that is generated by the project. This forms an important audit trail by such bodies as either customer or supplier quality assurance.

The quality file should contain the master copy of the product description, plus details of individual product test plans and the quality log. The project manager is responsible for setting up the quality file and quality log, and checking that either team managers or individuals are feeding information into the log.

Quality log

The quality log is a summary of tests carried out and test results. The initial entry is by the project manager when a stage plan is created. The team manager or individual adds the actual results as the quality checking is done.

Risk

Philosophy

It is not uncommon to hear people say 'This is a high risk project'. This statement by itself is of limited interest or value. We need far more detail. What are the actual risks? What are their causes? What is the probability of a risk occurring? How serious would the impact of that occurrence be? What can be done about it?

PRINCE2 suggests that you:

- Carry out risk assessment at the start of a project. Make proposals on what should be done about the risks. Get agreement on whether to start the project or not.
- Review the risks at the end of every stage. This includes existing risks that might have changed and new risks caused by the next stage plan. Get agreement on whether to continue into the next stage.
- Appoint an owner for every risk. Build into the stage plan the moments when the owners should be monitoring the risks. Check on the owners that they are doing the job and keeping the risk status up to date.
- Review every request for change for its impact on existing risks or the creation of a new risk. Build the time and cost of any risk avoidance or reduction, for example, into your recommendation on the action to be taken.
- Inspect the risks at the end of the project for any that might affect the product in its operational life. If there are any, make sure that you notify those charged with looking after the product. (Use the follow-on action recommendations for this.)

The project manager has the responsibility to ensure that risks are identified, recorded and regularly reviewed. The project board has two responsibilities:

- To notify the project manager of any external risk exposure to the project.
- To make decisions on the project manager's recommended reactions to risk.

It is good practice to appoint one individual as responsible for monitoring each identified risk, i.e. the person best placed to observe the factors that affect that risk. According to the risk, this may be a member of the project board, someone with project assurance duties, the project manager, the team manager or a team member.

Risk tolerance

Another name for this is 'risk appetite'. Before determining what to do about risks, a project must consider the amount of risk it is prepared to tolerate. A project may be prepared to take comparatively large risks in some areas and none at all in others. Risk tolerance can be related to the four tolerance parameters: risk to completion within timescale and/or cost, and to achieving product quality and project scope within the boundaries of the business case.

The organization's overall tolerance of exposure to risk must be considered, as well as a view of individual risks.

Although the management of risk is a cyclic process, it can be considered to have two main parts: risk analysis (the gathering of information about risks and the preparation of alternatives) and risk management (decision-making, taking action and watching what happens). These two parts are divided into the seven major activities shown in Figure 14.

The risk management process

Every project is subject to constant change in its business and wider environment. The risk environment is constantly changing too. The project's priorities and relative importance of risks will shift and change. Assumptions about risk have to be

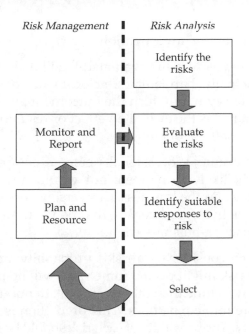

Figure 14 The major activities in the management of risk

regularly revisited and reconsidered, for example at each end stage assessment.

Risk analysis

Risk identification

This step identifies the potential risks (or opportunities) facing the project. It is important not to judge the likelihood of a risk at this early time.

Once identified, risks are all entered in the risk log. This is a summary document of all risks, their assessment, owners and status. The risk log is a control tool for the project manager, providing a quick reference to the key risks facing the project, what monitoring activities should be taking place and by whom.

Evaluation

Risk evaluation is concerned with assessing the probability and impact of individual risks, taking into account any interdependencies or other factors outside the immediate issue under investigation.

- *Probability* is the evaluated likelihood of a particular outcome actually happening (including a consideration of the frequency with which the outcome may arise).
- *Impact* is the evaluated effect or result of a particular outcome actually happening.

For example, occasional personal computer system failure is fairly likely to happen, but would not usually have a major impact on the business. Conversely, loss of power to a building is relatively unlikely to happen, but would have enormous impact on business continuity.

When considering a risk's probability, another aspect is when the risk might occur. Some risks will be predicted to be further away in time than others, and so attention can be focused on the more immediate ones. This prediction is called the risk's proximity. The proximity of each risk should be included in the risk log.

Identify suitable responses to risk

The actions break into broadly five types (Table 2).

Results of the risk evaluation activities are documented in the risk log. If the project is part of a programme, project risks

Table 2 Five responses to risk.

Prevention	Terminate the risk – by doing things differently and thus removing the risk, where it is feasible to do so. Countermeasures are put in place that either stop the threat or problem from occurring, or prevent it having any impact on the project or business
Reduction	Treat the risk – take action to control it in some way where the actions either reduce the likelihood of the risk developing or limit the impact on the project to acceptable levels
Transference	This is a specialist form of risk reduction where the impact of the risk is passed to a third party via, for instance, an insurance policy or penalty clause
Acceptance	Tolerate the risk – perhaps because nothing can be done at a reasonable cost to mitigate it, or the likelihood and impact of the risk occurring are at an acceptable level
Contingency	These are actions planned and organized to come into force as and when the risk occurs

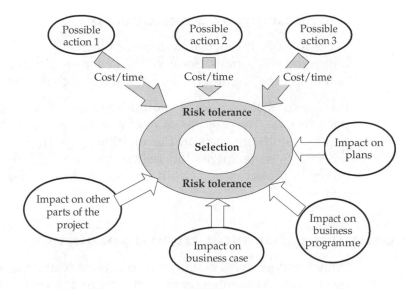

Figure 15 Risk action selection

should be examined for any impact on the programme (and vice versa). Where any cross-impact is found, the risk should be added to the other risk log.

Selection

This involves identification of a range of options for treating risks and selection of the most appropriate actions (Figure 15). For each possible action it is a question of balancing the cost of taking that action against the likelihood and impact of allowing the risk to occur.

The consideration has to be done in the light of the risk tolerances.

Risk management

Planning and resourcing

Having made the selection, the implementation will need planning and resourcing, and is likely to include plan changes and new or modified work packages.

Monitoring and reporting

There must be mechanisms in place for monitoring and reporting on the risk actions. Some of the actions may have only been to monitor the identified risk for signs of a change in its status.

Risks owned at team level should be reported on in the checkpoint reports. The project manager includes some form of report on any significant risks in the highlight report. The end stage report also summarizes the risk status. Where a risk actually occurs, a project issue should be used to trigger the necessary actions.

Budgeting for risk management

Whilst budget may be allocated to actions relating to risk treatment, such as contingency plans, there is often a failure to provide sufficient budget for the earlier parts of the process, such as risk assessment. Experience has shown that allocating the correct budget to the risk process early on will pay dividends later.

Mapping the risk management process to the P2 processes

At key points in a project, management of risk should be carried out (Figure 16).

Preparing a project brief (SU4)

The risk log needs to be created by this time. The project mandate may have referred to a number of risks facing the potential project. These may be such risks as competitor action, impending or mooted legislation, company policy changes, staff reorganization or cash-flow problems. The preparation of the project brief should cause an early study of such risks. Creation of the project approach may also have introduced some extra risks.

Authorizing initiation (DP1)

This is the first formal moment when the project board can examine the risk log as part of deciding whether project initiation

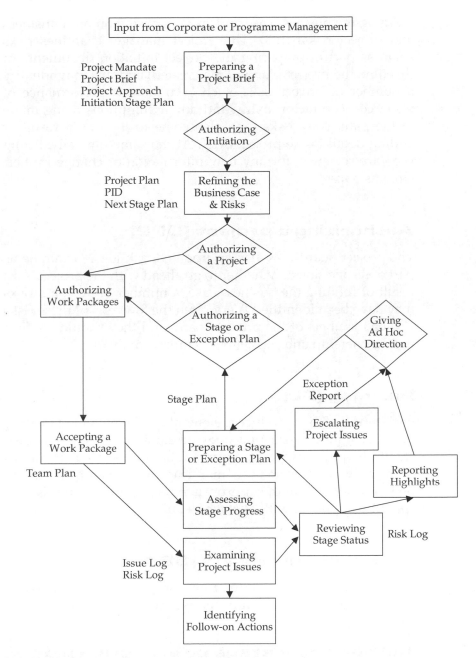

Figure 16 Map of the risk management process

can be justified. Pragmatically, the project manager should have discussed informally with board members any known risks that seem to threaten the project viability.

Refining the business case and risks (focusing on both business and project risks) (IP3). The project manager examines risks again as part of preparing the project initiation document. At this time the project plan will be created, and this may identify a number of project risks, such as unknown performance of resources, contractor ability and any assumptions being made in the plan. New risks may also come to light as a result of adding detail to the project brief. At the same time all existing risks are reviewed for any new information or change in their circumstances.

Authorizing a project (DP2)

The project board now has an updated risk log to examine as part of its decision on whether to go ahead with the project. As a result of refining the business case, a number of business risks may have been identified. Very often the 'owners' of these risks will be members of the project board, and they should confirm their ownership and the actions required of them.

Planning (PL)

Each time a plan is produced, elements of the plan may identify new risks, modify existing ones or eliminate others. No plan should be put forward for approval before its risk content has been analysed. This analysis may lead to the plan being modified in order to take the appropriate risk action(s). The risk log should be updated with all such details.

Updating the risk log (SB4)

As part of his preparation for a new stage, the project manager updates the risk log with any changes to existing risks.

Authorizing a stage or exception plan (DP3)

Before authorizing a plan, the project board has the opportunity to study the risk situation as part of its judgement of the continuing viability of the project.

Authorizing work package (CS1)

Negotiation with the team manager or team member may identify new risks or change old ones. It may require the project manager to go back and amend some part of the original work package or change the stage plan. Examples here are the assignee seeking more time or needing to change resources.

Accepting a work package (MP1)

This is the point when the team manager makes out a team plan to ensure that the products of the work package can be delivered within the constraints of the agreed work package. Like any other plan, it may contain new risks or modify existing ones.

Examining project issues (CS4)

Assessment of a new project issue may throw up a risk situation. This may stem from either the technical impact analysis or the business impact analysis. For example, the proposed change may produce a risk of pushing the stage or project beyond its tolerance margins.

Reviewing stage status (CS5)

This brings together the stage plan with its latest actual figures, the project plan, the business case, open project issues, the tolerance status and the risk log. The project manager (in conjunction with the project assurance roles) looks for risk situation changes as well as any other warning signs.

Escalating project issues (CS8)

As well as project issues, a risk change may cause the project manager to raise an exception report to the project board.

Reporting highlights (CS6)

As part of this task, the project manager may take the opportunity to raise any risk matters with the project board. Examples here would be notifying the board of any risks that are no longer relevant, warning about new risks, and giving reminders about business risks that board members should be keeping an eye on. The suggested format of a highlight report is included in the appendix to produce description outlines.

Giving ad hoc direction (DP4)

The project manager advises the project board of exception situations via the exception report. It has the opportunity to react with advice or a decision – for example, bringing the project to a premature close, requesting an exception plan, or removing the problem. The project board may instigate ad hoc advice on the basis of information given to it by corporate or programme management or another external source.

Identifying follow-on actions (CP2)

At the end of the project a number of risks may have been identified that will affect the product in its operational life. These should be transferred to the follow-on action recommendations for the information of those who will support the product after the project.

Change control

Philosophy

No matter how well planned a project has been, if there is no control over changes, this will destroy any chance of bringing the project in on schedule and to budget.

Overview

A project issue is the formal way into a project of any inquiry, complaint or request. It can be raised by anyone associated with the project about anything, for example:

- a desired new or changed function
- a failure of a product in meeting some aspect of the user requirements. In such cases the report should be accompanied by evidence of the failure and, where appropriate, sufficient material to allow someone to recreate the failure for assessment purposes
- a question about a possible misunderstanding
- a problem with a plan
- a failure of communication.

In other words, there is no limit to the content of a project issue beyond the fact that it should be about the project.

All possible changes should be handled by the same change control procedure. Apart from controlling possible changes, this procedure should provide a formal entry point through which questions or suggestions also can be raised and answered.

All project issues have to be closed by the end of the project or transferred to the follow-on action recommendations. The transfer of a project issue to these recommendations can only be done with the approval of the project board.

Request for change

A request for change records a proposed modification to the user requirements.

The request for change requires analysis to see how much work is involved. The cost of the identified work is assessed and the impact on the stage and project plans' budget and schedule assessed.

In order for the request for change to be implemented, it must be approved by either the project manager or the project board. Whose decision it is depends on the following:

- If it is not a change to a configuration item record that has already been *baselined* and the work can be done within the current stage plan's *tolerances*, the project manager can make the decision to implement it. Alternatively it can be passed to the project board for its decision. Since experience shows that there will be a lot of changes during the project, it is a good idea to make the project board decide on any changes other than trivialities.
- This keeps the board aware of how many changes are being requested and their cumulative impact on the schedule and cost. If the stage plan runs into trouble later, it is usually too late for the project manager to get any sympathy about a claim that lots of requests have been actioned without asking for more time or money. The answer will usually be: 'Why didn't you ask us? We could have cancelled or delayed some of them.'
- The decision must be made by the project board if the change is to one or more products that the project board has already been told are complete, more than anything, this is to retain the confidence level of the board. If it has been told that something is finished and later finds out that it has been changed without consultation, its sense of being in control evaporates.
- If the work to do the request for change cannot be done within the tolerance levels of the current stage plan, the decision on action *must* come from the project board. The project manager must submit an exception report with the request for change.

The project board's decision may be to:

- implement the change. If the change requires an exception plan, then this means approving the exception plan
- delay the change to an enhancement project after the current one is finished
- defer a decision until a later meeting
- ask for more information
- cancel the request.

The decision should be documented on the project issue and in the issue log.

Off-specification

An off-specification is used to document any situation where the product is failing to meet its specification in some respect.

As with requests for change, the decision on action is taken by either the project manager or project board. If the error is due to a failure within the project manager's responsibility, the onus is on the project manager to correct the problem within tolerances. Similarly, if the error is from a team manager's failure to fulfil an agreed work package, the onus is on the team manager (or the supplier if the team is from an external company) to correct the error without asking the project manager for more time or money.

Configuration management

No organization can be fully efficient or effective unless it manages its assets, particularly if the assets are vital to the running of the organization's business. A project's assets likewise have to be managed. The assets of the project are the products that it develops. The name for the combined set of these assets is a configuration. The configuration of the final deliverable of a project is the sum total of its products.

Within the context of project management the purpose of configuration management is to identify, track and protect the project's products as they are developed.

Configuration management is also the process of managing changes to the products. It implies that any version of the product and any revision of the components that make up the product can be retrieved at any time, and that the resulting product will always be built in an identical manner. Product enhancements and special variants create the need to control multiple versions and releases of the product. All these have to be handled by configuration management.

Baselines

Baselines are moments in a product's evolution when it and all its components have reached an acceptable state, such that they can be 'frozen' and used as a base for the next step. The next step may be to release the product to the customer, or it may be that you have 'frozen' a design and will now construct the sub-products.

A baseline is created for one of a number of reasons:

- to provide a sound base for future work
- as a point to which you can retreat if development goes wrong
- as an indication of the component and version numbers of a release
- as a bill of material showing the variants released to a specific site
- to copy the products and documentation at the current baseline to all remote sites
- to represent a standard configuration (e.g. product description) against which supplies can be obtained (e.g. purchase of personal computers for a group)
- to indicate the state the product must reach before it can be released or upgraded
- as a comparison of one baseline against another in terms of the products contained and their versions
- to transfer configuration items to another library, e.g. from development to production, from the supplier to the customer at the end of the project
- to obtain a report on what products of the baseline are not of status 'X'.

Status accounting and auditing

Configuration status accounting provides a complete statement of the current status and history of the products generated within the project or within a stage.

There are two purposes of configuration auditing. The first is to confirm that the configuration item records match reality. In other words, if my configuration item records show that we are developing version 3 of a product, I want to be sure that the developer has not moved on to version 5 without my knowing and without any linking documentation to say why versions 4 and 5 were created. The second purpose is to account for any differences between a delivered product and its original agreed specification. In other words, can the configuration item records trace a path from the original specification, through any approved changes, to what a product looks like now? These audits should verify that:

- all authorized versions of configuration items exist
- only authorized configuration items exist
- all change records, release records have been properly authorized by project management
- implemented changes are as authorized.

Product-based planning

I recommend product-based planning. There are two reasons for this. First, a project delivers products, not activities, so why begin at a lower level? The second reason is about quality. We can measure the quality of a product. The quality of an activity can only be measured by the quality of its outcome (the product).

Product-based planning has three components:

- product breakdown structure
- product descriptions
- Product flow diagram.

Product breakdown structure

A product breakdown structure is a hierarchy of the products that the plan requires to produce. At the top of the hierarchy is the final end product, e.g. a computer system, a new yacht, a department relocated to a new building. This is then broken down into its major constituents at the next level. Each constituent is then broken down into its parts, and this process continues until the planner has reached the level of detail required for the plan.

Let us take an example of a project whose objective is to procure a product. There are many complications that can occur in procurement, but for the sake of an example we shall keep this simple (Figure 17).

Another important departure from other methods is the emphasis that, apart from the technical products of a project,

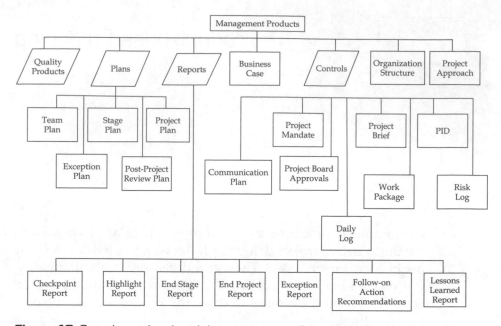

Figure 17 Sample product breakdown structure of management products

there are always management and quality products. Listing these will remind us that they, too, take effort to produce and need to be planned as much as the production of technical products.

The management and quality products are much the same for every project. Figure 18 is a sample product breakdown structure of management products. Quality products are expanded on in Figure 19.

Product description

For each identified product, at all levels of the product breakdown structure, a description is produced. Its creation forces the planner to consider if sufficient information is known about the product in order to plan its production. It is also the first time that the quality of the product is considered. The quality criteria indicate how much and what type of quality checking will be required (Figure 19).

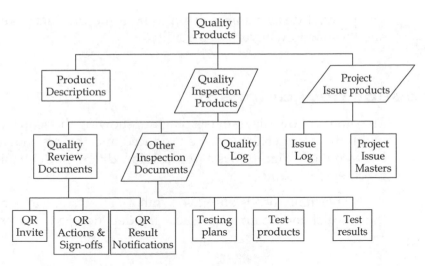

Figure 18 Example of a product flow diagram

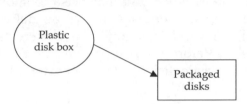

Figure 19 Product flow diagram for 'packaged disks'

The purposes of this are, therefore, to provide a guide:

- to the planner as to how much effort will be required to create the product
- to the author of the product as to what is required
- against which the finished product can be measured.

These descriptions are a vital checklist to be used at a quality check of the related products.

The description should contain:

- the purpose of the product
- the products from which it is derived
- the composition of the product
- any standards for format and presentation
- the quality criteria to be applied to the product
- the quality verification method to be used.

The product description is given to both the product's creator and those who will verify its quality.

Product flow diagram

The product flow diagram is a diagram showing the sequence in which the products have to be produced and the dependencies between them. Figure 20 is a product flow diagram (PFD) for the procurement example.

A PFD normally needs only two symbols: a rectangle to contain the product and an arrow to show the dependency.

External dependencies

There are times when you may wish to show that the plan is dependent on a product over whose delivery you have no control. For example, you might have to create a product 'packaged disks'. Before you can create this product you have to receive the plastic disk box from an external supplier. To show

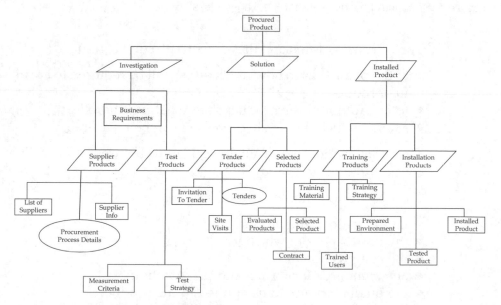

Figure 20 Product breakdown hierarchy

that the delivery of the product is outside your control you would use a different symbol. PRINCE2 suggests that you use an ellipse. The PFD for this example would be as shown in Figure 21.

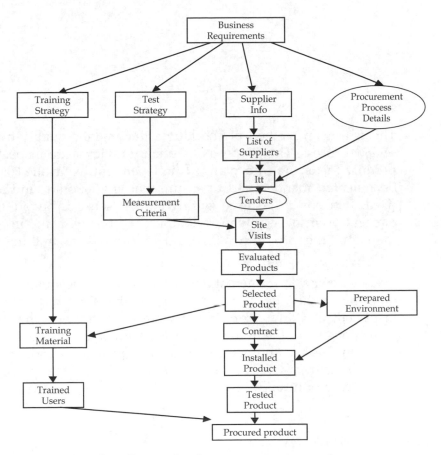

Figure 21 Product flow diagram for the procurement example

Quality review

This is a team method of checking a document's quality by a review process. The purpose of a quality review is to inspect a product for errors in a planned, independent, controlled and documented manner, and to ensure that any errors found are fixed. It needs to be used with common sense to avoid the dangers of an over-bureaucratic approach but with the intent to follow the procedures laid down (to ensure nothing is missed).

Quality review documentation, when filed in the quality file with the quality log, provides a record that the product was inspected, that any errors found were corrected and that the corrections were themselves checked. Knowing that a product has been checked and declared error-free provides a more confident basis from which to move ahead and to use that product as the basis of future work.

People involved

The interests of parties who should be considered when drawing up the list of attendees are:

- the product author
- those with project assurance responsibilities delegated by the project board
- the customer
- staff who will operate or maintain the finished product
- other staff whose work will be affected by the product
- specialists in the relevant product area
- standards representatives.

Roles at the quality review

There are four roles involved in a quality review:

- *The producer*, who is the author of the product being reviewed. This role has to ensure that the reviewers have all the required information in order to perform their job. This means getting a copy of the product from the configuration librarian to them during the preparation phase, plus any other documents needed to put it in context. Then the producer has to answer questions about the product during the review until a decision can be reached on whether there is an error or not. Finally, the producer will do most, if not all, of the correcting work. The producer must not be allowed to be defensive about the product.
- *The chairperson*, who is responsible for ensuring that the quality review is properly organized and that it runs smoothly during all of its phases.
- *The reviewer*, a person, or people, who either has a vested interest in the quality of the product or has the skills and experience necessary to assess the quality of the product.
- *A scribe*, someone to take notes of the actions identified at the meeting.

It must be remembered that these are roles. They must all be present at a quality review, but one person may take on more than one role.

Phases of the quality review procedure

There are three distinct phases within the quality review procedure: preparation, review and follow-up.

Phase 1: preparation

The objective of this phase is to examine the product under review and to create a list of questions for the review.

Each reviewer will study the product and supporting documents (including the quality criteria included in the product description), annotate the product and complete a quality review question list.

Phase 2: review

The objective of the review is to agree a list of any actions needed to correct or complete the product. The chairperson and the producer do not have to reconcile these actions at the meeting – it is sufficient for the chairperson and reviewer(s) to agree that a particular area needs correction or at least re-examination. Provided that the action is logged, the reviewers have an opportunity in the next phase to confirm that action has been taken.

Phase 3: follow-up

The objective of the follow-up phase is to ensure that all actions identified on the action list are dealt with.

When an error has been fixed, the producer will obtain sign-off from whoever is nominated on the action list. This person may be the reviewer who initially raised the query, but other reviewers have the option of checking the correction.

When all errors have been reconciled and sign-off obtained, the chairperson will confirm that the product is complete and sign off the action list. The documents will be filed in the quality file and the stage plan updated.

Formal and informal reviews

Quality reviews can be either formal (i.e. a scheduled meeting conducted as described above) or informal (i.e. a 'get-together' between two people to review informally a product). A variation on a formal review is to have the reviewers forward their action lists, but the actual review is done by only the chairperson and the producer.

Informal quality reviews will follow a similar format to the formal quality review – the paperwork emerging from both meetings is similar. The main difference will be the number of people involved, the informality of the proceedings during the three phases and the overall time required.

Part II

PRINCE2 revealed

The project mandate

When I think of some of the project mandates that I have seen, I am reminded of a line from a song in the musical *Kismet* – 'A fool sat beneath an olive tree, and a wondrous thought had he'. Sounds like another project mandate coming up!

The project mandate is supposed to be senior management's statement of what it wants the project to deliver. It should be a

beautifully clear, concise statement of requirements, leaving no uncertainty in the mind of the reader. Unfortunately it is very often a vague and very brief idea with no stated purpose for the project, constraints or reasons.

I was asked by the managing director (MD) of a yachting equipment firm to have a word with his project manager (note the singular!) about their project management methods, because he was concerned that projects always seemed to slide and progress information was not easy to get – the project manager was always too busy project managing to report to the MD (now where have we heard that before?). Interesting how the request came about; I was talking to the MD in the sauna of our local health centre. When I mentioned the kind of work I did, he jumped in immediately with his request, as though it had been at the top of his worry list for some time. I said that I would have a brief look just as a favour.

Anyway, off I went to chat to the project manager. The company was at the top end of the deluxe yacht market. Examples of their small projects were hatches for ocean-going yachts. It will come as no surprise to you to know that he was managing several small projects; in fact, all the engineering projects that the company had – and he was not about to delegate any project management to anyone. I asked to see a typical project mandate, and he pulled out of his drawer a memo from a salesman. The memo must have had no more than six lines, describing the customer's requirement in very general detail. From that the project manager dived into the project, no start-up, no initiation, no project organization, just the project manager and the team. I will say more about the yacht company's other project management methods later in this part. I wrote to the MD about my findings, but I never heard back from him. There is old saying that if you do not charge for something, it is regarded as being worth nothing, so I should not be too surprised that there was no follow-up.

Now back to project mandates in general. The project mandate most favoured by senior management is the verbal one where the words can mean almost anything, can be denied later or it can be implied that you misheard, and they get irritated if you ask questions, looking at you pityingly as if you are an imbecile. Project managers are supposed to be mind-readers who can write the Bible if given the first word ('Exodus!' – no, that's not it, you fool!). Some companies call it a vision statement. This often means that it does not have to touch reality. Some visions give the impression that a manager has seen something on *Star Trek*, gone ten light years past its technology and would like it next week, please.

A good project mandate should not need any improvement in order to become the project brief.

Appointing the executive

Programme management or senior management should appoint the executive. The idea is, senior managers, that you appoint someone you trust, give them the mandate and any constraints on such things as time and cost, and tell them to get on with it. Another part of this selection is ensuring that the executive has the necessary financial authority for the project's budget. Apart from progress reports, you should not expect to be asked for decisions unless something goes wrong or is forecast to exceed the limits that you set. That is 'management by exception' and it starts right at the top, otherwise you get involved in every decision that the project has to make, right down to the colour of ink cartridges to use. You might as well do the job yourself. Once you accept that delegation is a good thing, remember to delegate authority and responsibility that fit the job you have delegated.

I remember being asked to review the implementation of PRINCE2 in the Australian Department of Defence. The project managers, rather than senior management, had adopted PRINCE2 – not an unknown occurrence! Unfortunately, the early project boards had also been 'appointed' by the project managers, rather than by senior management. The result was that senior management did not feel that it had delegated the necessary authority to the project board, and therefore insisted on retaining the approval to move to the next stage until it had checked everything out. This resulted in delays of two to three months at every stage end.

That leads me to another point. If the project is important to senior management, it might be sensible to appoint one of them to be executive of the project. That should support the willingness to trust the executive.

I often get an interesting view on the executive role from candidate's answers in examinations. We set out a scenario that clearly shows who the project's sponsor is, with bags of authority and decision-making capability, and ask the candidate to design a project management team. Too often we get candidates saying things like, 'Bill Bloggs (the person we've set up for them as the sponsor) is so important that he can't be the executive. We'll put him down as "senior management" above the team'.

Appointing the project manager

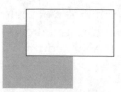

(Otherwise known as 'Who will take the blame?')

Another thing that I noticed when dealing with defence projects is that service men and women are rotated about every two years. So a five-year defence project would start and two years in the project manager is rotated to a fisheries protection ship, looking after cod, or is wing commander on an airfield in Boobalumbo. Two years later it all happens again. You cannot do that to a project without it suffering. You need the project manager to be there from start to finish – and ditto for the project board, at least for the executive. These are the main drivers of the project. If you keep taking away the driver, the vehicle is likely to crash!

Designing a project management team

Yes, I actually overheard a student say this to a colleague during a coffee break! I still chuckle at the memory. In my early days as a project manager there was a great deal of antagonism between the developer and the user or customer. Silly when you think of all the work that you can get the user to do: write product descriptions, attend quality reviews, confirm that the design is OK, make the tea...maybe that is going a bit too far. You read the phrase, 'Designing a project management team', in a few seconds. 'Yes', you say to yourself, 'I understand that'. OK, let us dig a bit deeper and see what questions you might have to ask in order to design the team.

Let us even go back to the appointment of the executive and project manager.

Executive

The executive should be appointed by corporate or programme management. If the project is regarded as critical or strategic, then the executive should be a member of corporate or programme management, and be able to:

- ensure the best level of communication between the two
- have knowledge of the most important elements as far as corporate or programme management are concerned and focus to ensure these are protected throughout the project
- provide the greatest level of confidence in the executive by corporate or programme management.

What if the project is a small, stand-alone project with no link to corporate or programme management? Who appoints the executive? In many small projects the sponsor, the person paying for the project, will appoint him/herself as executive. That is fine. It does mean that in such projects the top layer of PRINCE2's four layers of management is missing. So in these cases the executive has to set the project tolerances and decide on any issues that affect project-level tolerances. It is worth a check to ensure that this is the case if you can see no higher level of authority. I remember a case where a software house developed a system for a manager, on his authority. When the product was ready for installation, the controller of the large computer, on which it was due to run, objected. He had not been told about the system, had not planned it into the daily schedule, said there was not enough capacity on the computer (he was the final judge on what went onto his computer!) and rejected it. The system was never installed. You may say that this was the project manager's fault, but you can imagine how uncomfortable life became for the executive when the system did not appear on the computer and his/her management started asking questions. Again, this could have been avoided by asking the common-sense questions at the outset – 'Whose commitment do we need?'

Project manager

Has this person been appointed by corporate or programme management, by the executive, by the customer or by the supplier? Will this have any impact on the ability of the project manager to direct, manage and control the project staff? Is the project manager experienced and skilled in project management and in the method to be used? The London Stock Exchange's style is to appoint a manager from the exchange floor, in other words, a manager from the area that will use the final product. They overcome the lack of project management and PRINCE2 knowledge by having a project management group, experts who assist and guide the project manager throughout the project. This works extremely well. One benefit to the company is that the project manager is committed 100 per cent (or more!) to the project. Also the project management team gets a very good, rounded understanding of senior management's needs across a wide variety of projects, and ensures that there is consistency across all projects. While we are on the subject of using such groups as a project management support team, this is the ideal recipient of a lessons learned report – to incorporate any lessons into the project management standards and ensure they are adopted by all other projects. Since they are advising all project managers, this is easy to do.

Do you need to identify the senior user(s) first, in order to ensure that a project manager is chosen who is acceptable to the senior user(s)?

If you remember the story I told under 'Project mandate' about the small yachting equipment firm, you will recall that the company had only one Project Manager. It did not take me long during our conversation to realize that this was a man who enjoyed carrying the world's burdens on his shoulders – as long as he could act the martyr and tell you how hard he worked, chasing all the projects around. The last thing he was prepared to do was to delegate – certainly none of the management aspects; those were the perks of his job, and he did not want any competition from anyone else. He would simply take on every new project with a long-suffering sigh. He was drowning (good for someone from a yachting company, eh!) in work, but the results were of secondary importance to feeding his ego. The example will crop up elsewhere in the book.

Senior supplier

Many projects are purchasing contracts, where one of the jobs of the project is to find one or more suppliers. If the suppliers are unknown at the start, they cannot be filling the senior supplier role. Do we manage without one, or do we look for an internal purchasing or contracts manager (or whoever will be responsible for negotiations with potential suppliers) and appoint that person as senior supplier? If we do, then we may keep that person in that role throughout the project, or it may make more sense to swap to the real supplier(s) once they are appointed. Remember, PRINCE2 offers the chance to review the project management team appointments at every stage end. If you can see this coming, why not make that point the end of a stage for that reason?

How many senior suppliers do you want? Each project's circumstances will guide you to a sensible decision, but you certainly do not want many. Can you have one senior supplier with other less important suppliers under contract to the main supplier? There may be several suppliers with no link to each other, but do you need all of them to be senior supplier? The key question here is, 'Do they need to be on the project board in order to contribute to joint decisions?' Not every supplier should be on the project board. The real key is the size of the commitments and decisions that they have to make. If they simply provide a small service, then they are just a resource and dealt with by means of a work package. One mistake to avoid is appointing a senior supplier on the assumption that they will be responsible for commitments from all other suppliers, even those with whom they have no contact and share no common products. This would be nonsense in real life, and as we keep saying, PRINCE2 is structured common sense, so if common sense tells you that a particular responsibility or connection is ridiculous, then you are misusing PRINCE2.

A PRINCE2 Practitioner examination concerned the creation of a company brochure for customers. Products required included glossy paper and professional photographs. The project also needed a quote from the local post office for bulk mailing. It was amazing how many candidates came back and suggested that the stationer, photographer and post office manager would share the senior supplier role. Can you imagine them attending end stage assessments? Even worse was a suggestion by some that the stationer, who was a dynamic individual, would be the senior supplier and represent the post office and photographer. What chance of his being able to make commitments on behalf of the other two?

One error that I often find among candidates answering an examination question about what a project's organization should be is that they will appoint someone because 'they are enthusiastic' or 'know a lot about the subject'. These are not reasons to appoint someone to a project board role. A project board role is all about decision-making and commitment. If the person cannot commit the required resources, he or she is not a candidate for a project board role.

Senior users

A similar question here – how many does the project need? Remember, you do not want those who have opinions, you want those who make the decisions and commitments. (It is the same in my home. I have opinions, my wife makes the decisions and I end up with the commitment.) If there are many contenders for the role, can they be harmonized into a user committee with a chairperson who will be the senior user?

Sometimes company politics get in the way; sometimes there are genuine sets of users with quite different needs; sometimes you need commitment of user resources that you cannot get from just one person.

Has the senior user already been appointed by programme management to keep an eye on the interests of the programme's users?

The project board and authorizing changes

One of the key responsibilities of the project board is to authorize any changes. This is reasonable. The project board authorizes the project based on the specification written in the project initiation document. If anything is to be changed or added to that specification (or the acceptance criteria or project approach), then you should go back to the board that gave you the money and resources to do the project and ask if it is acceptable to make the change. The project board will consider the impact on budget, time, business case and risks, and give you its answer. All very nice in theory, but what happens if the project receives hundreds of change requests? Have the members of the project board got the time to spare to consider them all? There are many projects that do get hundreds of change requests. If you consider the software that looks after National Health Insurance, this is an example of a maintenance 'project' that receives change requests because of legislative changes, changes caused by test cases, apart from many requests to improve the facilities, ease of use, additional terminals, printers, servers, etc. A similar project is the one to support Job Seeker's Allowance. When this project began, legislation was still passing through Parliament, so the specification continued to change for months after work had started. In such situations, could the project board give the time to study and decide on so many changes? No, it appointed a change authority to do the job. The representation was the same as the project board – the business, user and supplier interests. The project board gave the change authority a budget to pay for changes, together with a couple of limitations. There are usually a maximum amount of this budget that can be spent in any one stage and a maximum amount for any single change. Any potential breach of one of these limits has to be referred to the project board.

Project assurance

Will any or all members of the project board do their own assurance? Are they capable of doing the job and do they have the time? If the project is part of a programme, have programme assurance roles been created that will either do the assurance job for your project or have to liaise with any project assurance roles?

If the senior user's assurance role is intent on checking supplier plans to see if the quality checking is adequate and on getting involved with those quality checks, has all this been spelt out in the contract with the supplier? It can save lots of arguments later.

Many PRINCE2 students only think of user assurance. The task of assuring the work for the senior supplier is also important, especially if there are any penalty clauses for errors in the final product. It is more usual in projects to find that the supplier has staff concerned with checking quality, than to find these on the customer's staff.

The executive also has assurance responsibilities that are often overlooked. How is the business case looking? What is the impact on it of a major change request that has been submitted? What does the business case look like now that we have finished another stage? What external events are happening that might have an impact on the business case? These are all questions for the executive's assurance role.

Will the skills needed for assurance change from stage to stage? Quite likely in a project using new technology – so perhaps some of the assurance roles should be reallocated, or at least reconsidered at each stage end.

I remember in the days of PRINCE® before it became PRINCE2™ I was advising a group of government people on how to form a project assurance team for the senior user. Some software was being developed for the government by a combination of a computer company and a consultancy group. I discussed with the project assurance team the need to review the developers' plans with particular emphasis on where and how quality was checked, to confirm that the design would meet the specification, and to get involved in the quality checking process or to identify other users who would do this. When it came to it, they did not do any of these things. Result – the suppliers delivered; the product failed its user acceptance test. It went back to the suppliers and when it was resubmitted, it failed again. 'It doesn't meet our requirements' – 'Oh, yes, it does', 'Oh, no, it doesn't'. The customer sued for the return of the payments it had made. The supplier sued for the remainder of the money. The system was never used, and only the lawyers won. It is too late to find out in final testing that the product is not what you thought you were getting. The job of user and supplier assurance is to ensure throughout the project life that the specification is good, the design meets the specification and the developed product meets the design.

If there is more than one person charged with project assurance – and here I'm talking of project assurance for all three project board roles – how will they be organized? Will they all work independently? Will they work as a team? If so, who will lead that team?

Project assurance and quality assurance

An incredible number of people confuse project assurance with quality assurance, so let us make the difference clear. Project Assurance is a PRINCE2 term (hence the capital initial letters). Each member of the project board has assurance responsibilities, which they may choose to delegate. Quality assurance is company-wide, not within a project. It is usually a group, charged with creating and maintaining the company's quality management system and ensuring that its standards are used properly throughout the company's work. It is this last part that may bring about an overlap of the two roles. In pursuit of its overall check on use of the standards, quality assurance will require to check that a project is using the relevant standards correctly – and that the standards are effective. The senior user and senior supplier may, therefore, decide to appoint a member of the quality assurance group to perform all or part of their project assurance role. But if you are talking about a PRINCE2 role, it is project assurance, not quality assurance.

Project assurance and the processes

Where should project assurance get involved? Many examination candidates make the mistake of believing that project assurance gets involved in sub-process DP3, 'authorizing a stage'. That is far too late. Before then, project assurance should have been monitoring all the work leading up to the end stage assessment, i.e. have been involved in all the SB sub-processes; creating the next stage plan (checking that sufficient quality checks are planned, advising on quality reviewers), updating the project plan and business case, updating the risk log, etc. By the time 'authorizing a stage' comes around, any problems should have been sorted out.

Project assurance must be involved in the creation of stage and team plans, poking their noses in and insisting on the level of quality checking, the timing of quality checking and the resources to be used.

There is also a job for project assurance (user and supplier in particular) in the PL process. In PL2, where product-based planning is used, they should check product descriptions, confirming that the users were involved in defining the purpose, composition and quality criteria. The quality-checking method and the quality-checking skills required should also have input from project assurance.

CS1 and MP1 are other sub-processes where project assurance should be involved, checking out the work package, checking the quality check attendees in the team plan, ensuring that staff planned to take part in quality inspections have been trained in the necessary techniques.

In MP2 project assurance will check that the quality checking is done correctly, and that the quality log is updated with the results. If someone from quality assurance has a project assurance role, they will also be checking that the quality inspection method used is satisfactory for the job.

Project assurance should be involved in CS4, 'examining project issues', looking at the impact on project scope, costs, schedule, the business case, risks and so on. If the approval of changes is a project board responsibility, it needs input from its project assurance on the impact of potential changes before approving or rejecting them.

Team managers

Team managers are optional! That means that small projects are unlikely to need them. You will still use the role, but it will be combined with the project manager role. In a small project the project manager will negotiate work packages with individual team members.

Will your project have team managers? If they are from external suppliers, what type of contract do you have with them? To whom does the contract say they report? Could there be any problems in them taking direction from you? If there are internal teams, are the people dedicated full time to the project or part time? If part time, what agreement do you have with their normal manager to allow you to plan use of their time with confidence that they will be available? Do you have staff allocated to the project, or do you have to agree work packages with a line manager, who then decides who will do the work for your project? If you work in this environment, it is simplest to regard the line manager as the senior supplier, making commitments that he/she will find the relevant resources. If the work packages are for individuals, but the line manager decides who will perform the work, then use the line manager as the team manager as well as senior supplier.

One classic mistake that those new to PRINCE2 make is to imagine that if an external source is planned to provide a service or product to the project, there must be a team manager from that source. Imagine that your project is to create a company calendar and you need a stationer to provide samples of glossy paper for it. In real life, would you try to appoint a person from the stationers as a team manager, or would you simply write out a product description for the paper samples and go and get them?

Many newcomers to PRINCE2 read about external products in product-based planning, team managers in the organization component, put the two together – and hey presto! Every product bought in by a project is regarded as an external product, and this means that there must be a team manager! Wrong thinking; if your project buys a product from a shop, such as a stapling machine, this does not need the shopkeeper to be appointed as a team manager.

If the project uses an external organization to build products for the project, this will require a team manager to be appointed, and this person will usually be supported (and controlled) by the senior supplier role. This is the role that will commit the resources of the team manager and the external team to each stage plan.

Remember that the teams required by a project may change as the project moves through its cycle. The team required to design a product may not be the team required to build it. When it comes time to plan the next stage of a project, this is one reason why there may need to be changes to the project management team.

Project management team

This brings me to another point that is not well understood. In PRINCE2 the project management team consists not only of the project board and the project manager. It also contains the project assurance, team manager and project support roles.

Appointing project support

Is your project part of a programme? If so, how are changes controlled – at a programme level? There will at least be a need for liaison across all the projects of the programme. How will you handle configuration management? Is the project so small that a team member can handle it as a part-time job? Does the project need a full-time configuration librarian? I was talking recently to the configuration librarian for the PRINCE2 Practitioner examinations. He reckoned that to handle a project issue to make even a minor change to a scenario, question or marking scheme required one hour of his time. We now have PRINCE2 examination questions translated into several languages, and configuration management has the task of keeping them all in line with each other. Does the customer insist on a specific configuration management method or tool being used? When the final product is handed over, does the customer have a particular configuration method into which your products have to fit? Do you have a central project support office that provides configuration management expertise and tools to all projects? How will you handle change control? Does the company have a standard procedure and set of forms for changes, or do you need to staff and train this function for your project? How will you handle the general administration tasks, such as filing, travel arrangements?

Is there a central group offering expertise in use of a planning tool or in risk management? If so, someone from this group may need to be allocated a role in the project support function on your project.

Appointing a project management team

> Can we remove the word 'responsibility' from my role description?

The main task of this process is to discuss the role with the individual and agree to it. The easy way to do this is to begin with a copy of the standard role description from Appendix B in the PRINCE2 manual. That way you do not forget any responsibilities or tasks. If a person objects to a task, it can be moved to another role – providing that whoever takes that other role agrees! The aim is not to shift all responsibilities onto the shoulders of the project manager! The aim is to stick as closely as possible to the standard role descriptions unless there is a very good reason to change. One reason for modifying a standard role would be that two or more people are to share that role and the role needs tailoring to the specific area that will be covered by each sharer. A responsibility or task may be moved, but it should not be dropped. Someone has to do it, however small the project.

Having got agreement, the role description should be changed into a job description with any changes from the standard plus the name of the person to whom it is allocated. Two copies should be printed, both signed by the role-taker. That person keeps one copy. The other is filed in the project file. In very small projects all this formality may be unnecessary, but it is a wise precaution to at least ensure that all involved have seen the description of the standard role that they are taking.

If the project management team changes for any reason, any new people or those changing roles have to go through the procedure again.

It is always useful in large projects to circulate, to all those in the communication plan, details of the project management team structure and signed job descriptions. Then everyone knows who is responsible for what.

It would be nice if all project board members had a background of project management, but this is not always the case. I have come across cases of project boards whose standard approach to a plan is to insist on cuts in the cost and time on the assumption that the project manager will have padded it out. It then becomes a game of who can bluff the other. It seems to me that one sensible use of project assurance would be to have an experienced project manager who can be trusted by the project board to examine a proposed plan on its behalf.

Writing a project brief

The aim of the project brief is to fill in all the gaps in the information provided by the project mandate. Remember, in PRINCE2 philosophy, the project manager has no control over the project mandate. It is normally created before the project manager is appointed. If the project mandate has all the information that you need, then it becomes the project brief and you can move on to the other work of 'starting up a project'.

When the project manager is appointed, it is a human reaction for the project manager to want to please senior management and agree to dash into developing the product – without any of this 'bureaucracy' of checking what information about the project the project mandate contains and 'wasting' time writing out a project brief. But have a look at the product description of the project brief. There is not any information there that you do not need before you start. Let us have a look at a template that you can use for a project brief.

A project brief template

Introduction (not obligatory in the PRINCE2 manual)

The purpose of this section is to describe the project brief itself. It will include a statement of the general reasons for producing a brief, as well as a project specific description of its purpose.

The reasons for the level of detail in the document should be given. The level may depend on how much information is available at the time of producing the brief, or it may depend on the level requested. A very small or low risk project will require less detail than a major or strategic project.

Background

The purpose of this section is to put the project in context by describing where it fits in the scheme of things. It will contain a brief high level description of the background to the project and relevant historical and strategic information.

There should be a brief statement of the problem/opportunity/requirement that the project is to address, and an indication of how it fits with the business strategy.

References should be made to existing documentation rather than reproducing it.

Project definition

This section explains what the project needs to achieve, what the boundaries are, plus any relationships that are needed.

Project objectives

The purpose of this paragraph is to state the objectives of the *project*, which should not be confused with the objectives of the products it is to deliver.

For example,

the objectives of the new PC project are:

To make available a standard, cost effective pc configuration to customers by 31 January 1999;

To put in place a procurement method that takes advantage of the standardization to reduce prices and delivery times.

In order to do this, the project will deliver the products described below.

Project scope

What are the boundaries of the product? How does it relate to other products?

Outline project deliverables

Identify the major product(s) that will be created, modified, obtained or removed by the project.

Exclusions

It may be necessary to state the things that the project will not create, modify, obtain or remove, if a reasonable assumption could be made that the project will, in fact, include them.

Constraints

The purpose of this paragraph is to describe the constraints within which the project must operate. Constraints such as those listed below should be identified:

- limitations imposed by management
- implementation or other fixed dates
- limitations on the skill/training of users of the final product, e.g. if designing a new mobile phone
- recognition of financial year or tax year

- ministerial decree
- competitor actions
- limit on resources
- limit on costs.

Any restrictions (either management or technical) on the project's freedom to manoeuvre must be recorded.

Project interfaces

The purpose of this paragraph is to describe the things upon which the project will depend *during its life cycle*. Dependencies of other projects upon this project as well as the dependencies of this project on other projects should be included.

If the project is dependent on external products, then they must be identified and monitored. Since there is no direct control over these external products some means of monitoring their progress or availability must be established and described here. For each external product required by the project as much of the following information as is currently available should be identified:

- the product name
- the project products dependent on it
- who is responsible for supplying or producing it
- when it is expected
- when it is required.

As well as products, you should consider such things as:

- conformance to existing operational standards
- conformance to existing functions and procedures
- release of staff from another project
- policy formulation from another area of the business
- conformance to strategies and standards
- customer and supplier management interfaces.

Product interfaces

This is a description of the interdependencies that will exist between the project's products after they have been delivered and those of other projects, operational products or line management functions.

Other projects may depend on the products of this project. These interdependencies should also be identified.

Outline business case

The purpose of this section is to document the justification for the project. It will be based upon the underlying business problem or opportunity that the project is to address.

Any information known or mandated about the timescale, effort and cost objectives of the project should be stated.

For large, high-risk projects, a cost/benefit analysis and investment appraisal showing costs, benefits and cash flow for the project may have been created in some earlier study. If so, they should be included here.

For smaller, low risk projects, a simple statement of why the project is required may suffice.

If there is a separate document containing the business case, say from a feasibility study, then a summary or a reference to it will be sufficient.

Customer's quality expectations

Benefits may accrue from simply delivering the products or, more likely, they will only materialize through operation of the products.

The purpose of this section is to define overall quality expectations by describing criteria that will be used to judge the quality of the project and its products. Criteria should be measurable against some kind of yardstick.

Examples of criteria include:

- delivered on time
- delivered to cost
- productivity
- functional requirements met
- accepted by customer
- product performance

- reliability
- maintainability
- user friendliness
- security and control.

Any known risks?

The purpose of this section is to list and describe any known key risks to the project or the business case and to indicate, where possible, the countermeasures needed to eliminate or minimize their impact. There may be risks embedded in the project mandate, a lack of some information, a suspect business case, unknown costs, an unreliable or old 'project plan' from a previous feasibility study, the project approach or the staff to be used.

The overall risk to which the implemented product, or lack of it, exposes the company should also be made clear.

Project plan (not part of the current PRINCE2 manual product description)

There may be an estimate of project duration and cost from a previous study. If so, it should be confirmed as achievable before inclusion in this brief.

Project tolerances (not part of the project brief product description in the current PRINCE2 manual)

Senior management should indicate to the executive what tolerance is to be allowed the total project in terms of budget and schedule. If there is no earlier estimate of duration and cost, senior management may not yet have set the tolerances. This should be stated and tolerances established as part of the project brief by the executive.

Acceptance criteria

See the next chapter.

It is difficult to write good acceptance criteria. Here are a few words that might help.

- All criteria are dependent on all others.
- Arbitrary definition of one may preclude meeting others, e.g. short development time and high reliability.
- If you ignore a critical criterion completely, you can artificially achieve any level of any other criterion, e.g. cost and quality, speed of development and quality.
- Criteria need to be prioritized. Classify the criteria as mandatory or desirable (give a rating of 1–10, low to high).
- A mandatory criterion may also appear as desirable (see later examples).
- It will take several passes to come up with a consistent set of criteria.

Table 3 is an example of a set of acceptance criteria for a small IT system a few years ago. It contains an example of a criterion (cost) that appears both as a mandatory requirement and as a 'nice-to-have' feature.

Auditing acceptance criteria

- Are they related to the decision (acceptance of the final product) to be made?
- Are there duplications?
- Are the 'musts':

  - really mandatory?
  - measurable?
  - realistic?

- Are two criteria combined as one?
- Are any alternatives embedded in the criteria?
- Are the criteria sufficiently specific?
- Are the weightings accurate?
- Is the list balanced?

Table 3 Example set of criteria for a small IT system.

Description	Requirement Priority	Alternative Value	Note Score
Cost			
Maximum £10 000	M		
As little as possible	8		
Target date 1 May	M		
Installation locations – Head Office	M		
Mandatory equipment – current company PC	M		
Expansion			
All camps in year 2 on stand-alone PCs	M		
On-line link to H.O. PC	6		
Performance			
Response times – average response <2 seconds	M		
Capable of being run by present level of staff	M		
Maximum of 1 day's training	8		
Availability 9–5 Monday–Friday	M		
Reliability			
Backup safeguards for data in place on installation	M		
Mean time between failures			
1 in first 3 months	8		
1 per year thereafter	10		
Mean time to repair 4 hours	8		
Quality			
All calculations to be accurate once installed	10		
Automatic recovery from keying errors	9		
Standards to be used – PRINCE2	M		

Project approach

I am amazed – and alarmed – by how many PRINCE2 examination candidates do not really understand what the project approach is. Many confuse it with a customer's quality expectations, the project brief, the project quality plan or some sort of textual project plan. It is none of these. It is a statement of the approach to be taken to the provision of a solution. If there was a previous feasibility study, this should have said what the approach would be, e.g. 'We are going to buy component X from company Y and modify our products A and B to interface with it' or 'This is an in-house development that is part of programme X and will use the equipment and tools specified by the programme'.

Now there is no question that the type of project approach will affect the customer's quality expectations and the project quality plan. If you buy a component off the shelf, you are too late to inspect its specification and design quality. In many cases you have little chance of inspecting its quality during production by the supplier. You can only check what other customers think of the product's quality and put the product through some tests on receipt. Your quality expectations might be a little less for a mass-produced product, but you may be balancing that against not having to spend a lot of time and a lot of money on developing your own. If your project is part of a programme, the programme will no doubt provide your project approach, especially if your project is not the first in the programme.

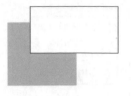

Configuration management

> Now let's call the whole dinner 'product A.'
> It consists of A1, the meat products, and A2, the vegetable products.
> A1 consists of A1.1, the lamb chop, and A1.2, the gravy.
> A2 consists of A2.1, the peas...

> Mum, can I have some more A1.2 please?

> He's been like this since he became Configuration Librarian

> Here's version 3.1 of the custard

Configuration management is regarded as a boring subject, but it affects the quality of the project work and, if it is done badly, it can kill any hopes that you had of a successful project. I once visited a software house that had a good configuration management package. They used a quotation that I felt summed up the need and reason for configuration management:

> If your project has more than one product, more than one version of a product and more than one person working on the

project, then you are doing configuration management. It's just a question of how well you're doing it.

I remember an oil company needing to add a new offshore oilrig's output to the pipe that brought ashore all the oil from the various offshore rigs. When it looked for the blueprints of the current pipeline, it found that these were spread across three different sites, hundreds of miles apart; some were missing and there was a suspicion that for many of the blueprints found, the one they had was not the latest version. So they had to go down to the sea bed and map it all again at a cost of £2 million. Failure to do configuration management can be very expensive!

At the APM Group we had a need for a configuration management method to control the Practitioner examination papers. An examination paper consists of a scenario and three questions, selected from a database of up to twelve questions, enabling us to reuse that scenario many times without repeating the same set of questions. There are possibly up to two attachments, each providing some extra information for a particular question, a marking scheme and marking guidelines for each question, a feedback form for examination failures and a feedback form for the training organization on what topics in the examination were handled badly by the candidates. The various parts of the examination may be given to different individuals or groups to create or revise. The whole thing would go through three or four revision cycles and be tested by up to three trainers before being used. Clearly, this involved lots of documents, lots of linkage information, several versions of everything and many people working on them, plus a need to compile various documents when approved into an examination paper. Below is the configuration management plan that we came up with to keep all of this under control – the names have been changed to protect the guilty!

Configuration management plan for PRINCE2 Practitioner papers

Practitioner papers are now developed over a period of many weeks, and have input from several sources – the author, the Exam Panel, trainers who comment on them and candidates who test them. A practitioner paper consists of a scenario, questions, attachments, marking scheme, marking guidelines, a candidate feedback form and ATO guidelines. The same scenario may be used in many papers with different questions, attachments and marking schemes. Each paper is studied in the light of the answers given by the first batch of candidates to answer them, and may be amended as a result. Thus the papers will pass through a number of versions before being finalized and work on the various parts may be delegated to a number of people. When a paper reaches a solid baseline, it is then translated into various foreign languages. All of these points emphasize the need for a comprehensive configuration management method.

Responsibilities

Gordon Bennett, as Chief Examiner will hold the development libraries.

Eileen Dover (the writer of that famous cliff tragedy!) will hold the library of live papers and be responsible for their issue to ATOs for examinations. She will also put them on the web site for access by the examiners, including those in the Netherlands and Australia.

Lydia Teapot will hold a master set of general questions and their marking scheme templates.

Method

There will be a master folder for each scenario. In the master folder there will be:

- a file of the scenario
- a matrix file showing the combinations of questions and attachments for an examination paper
- a folder containing all scenario questions. There will be separate files in the folder for the question, its marking scheme, marking guidelines and its portion of the ATO feedback form
- a folder containing all attachments
- a folder for each variation, i.e. Practitioner paper. The folder will contain two files, one labelled 'ATO', which will contain the scenario, three questions and any relevant attachments; the other labelled 'Examiners', which will hold the same information as the ATO file, plus the collated marking scheme, marking guidelines, candidate feedback form and ATO feedback form

- a file of build instructions for each variation of the paper, i.e. different combinations of questions
- an archive folder for old versions of any of these products
- a project issues folder for all change suggestions/actions.

Header information

Each scenario, question and attachment will contain the following information in its name and header:

- scenario identifier
- name
- version
- owner
- status.

Additionally, each question will identify the type of question, i.e. analytical, contextual or theoretical.

Each scenario, question and attachment will contain the following information in its footer:

- date
- reason for change, linking to the project issue that contains the reason for the change from the previous version.

In the matrix each variation will have a version number, status and reason for change.

Other information

Each question will begin with a statement of the attachments to the scenario that it requires.

Naming convention

The naming convention for folders is

Nxnnvv

where N stands for new manual, x = either S for a project at its start, M for a scenario based in the middle of a project or C for a scenario about bringing a project to its close; nn is a serial number beginning at 01; vv is the variation number indicating the scenario with a particular combination of three questions and attachments.

Questions and attachments will have an identifier Q or A, a two-digit serial number and will include a version number.

Version numbering

Each element will start at version 0. Changes to this will start at 0.1 and continue until the document is baselined, when it will become version 1. If this has to be changed, changes will begin at 1.1. When that document is baselined it will change to version 2, and so on.

Filing and retrieval security

All those with responsibility for Practitioner files will take weekly backups onto another medium. Gordon Bennett and Eileen Dover will archive old versions onto a backup medium as soon as any examinations using the old versions have been marked. Each scenario folder will contain an archive folder. This will contain all superseded documents.

PRINCE2 says that the business case should be the driving force of a project. If a project cannot be justified in terms of its benefit to the organization, it should not be started – or if it has started and later that justification disappears or reduces to the point where the project cost and effort are greater than the benefits, the project should be stopped. Justification of a project is not the job of the project manager. It is the job of the executive. Very often the executive may ask the senior user role to contribute to reasons and financial justification. The project manager should be ready to advise the project board on possible inclusions, things to consider, but should ensure that he/she only makes suggestions and that decisions on what goes in the business case are firmly in the court of the executive.

If any project fails to achieve its claimed benefits, the documentation should show that the benefits were not from the fevered imagination of the project manager. The project manager's main task is to ensure that sanity prevails in the claimed benefits. I was once on a team in a subsidiary company of a very large firm. The team developed an ordering and invoicing system for their subsidiary that could be used by all subsidiaries. They offered it around in return for paying a share of the development costs. The share reduced as more subsidiaries adopted it. One subsidiary put forward a case for redeveloping its own system. A half-trained systems analyst could have driven a coach and horses through its business case, but it came to the same conclusion that its senior managers wanted for political reasons, so off they went. About £500 000 later their system still was not working and twenty other subsidiaries had taken the system originally offered around – by now for a lot less money. Headquarters finally ordered the subsidiary to come into line and take the offered system. This was followed in that subsidiary by a lot of hunting for the guilty parties. The business case bore the name of the project manager, so no guesses as to who got the blame.

One of the big problems with business cases is in finding measurements that can be applied to the claimed benefits.

How is the executive going to check whether a benefit has been obtained, and to what extent? The trouble here is that you have to think of how to measure success when the business case is being refined in 'initiating a project'. It is too late to start thinking of how to measure when you are 'closing a project'. Before you start a project, you have to ensure that measurements have been taken of the existing situation, against which the results of the project can be checked. What is today's product costing? How many staff does it take? How fast (or slow) is it? What is the turn-round time? What are the old product's problems? How will you measure improvement? These are difficult questions for the executive and the users, and the danger is that they will come up with vague statements that cannot be quantified – like those in the 'measurable business benefits' cartoon.

One oil company for which I worked needed a new payroll system, and it came out with a nice measurement, 'the new payroll should cost no more than 3p per member of staff to run', which was fine in an environment that had an algorithm for calculating computer time and peripheral usage costs.

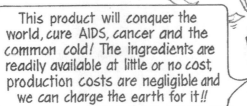

This product will conquer the world, cure AIDS, cancer and the common cold! The ingredients are readily available at little or no cost, production costs are negligible and we can charge the earth for it!!

DON'T LET THE USER EXAGGERATE THE BUSINESS BENEFITS

Project issues

Project issues and the issue log

The issue log is set up in process IP5, 'setting up project controls'. This seems very neat. It fits in with the other control documents created at this time, and normally project issues do not start rolling in until we hit the process 'controlling a stage' for the first time. But remember, PRINCE2 is flexible. If, by chance, an issue should come up in the early parts of initiating a project (for example, when putting together the project quality plan, you discover a conflict between the customer and supplier standards, or there is a clash between the quality required, the time constraint and the project plan), or even during the process, 'starting up a project', you do not turn round and say, 'sorry, this can't be a project issue because I haven't reached that sub-process yet'. If you are a PRINCE2 site, you should have a standard project issue form on file – and probably a blank issue log, or at least a template for one. You simply bring the action of creating the issue log forward, make out the project issue and deal with it in the normal way.

Project issues and risks

Remember that the first entry for any information on concerns, questions or problems is through a project issue. If there is some information that will lead to a risk, it comes in via a project issue. Now, whatever happens to this information, it has been recorded. The sub-process CS4, 'examining project issues', is where the decision is made that a project issue has discovered a risk. The risk is then entered onto the risk log. This may sound pedantic, but the project issue procedure ensures

149

that the original source is advised that the information has been received and is being acted upon. The project issue can be closed off with a note to say that it has been transferred to the risk log. The source is told that, and everyone is happy. If those with small projects think that this smells of too much bureaucracy, remember that PRINCE2 allows you to handle things verbally. But think, do you want (or need) a written record of where advice of a risk came from?

Quality

When I was in charge of project management standards at an oil company I asked the assistant general manager who was responsible for quality in our projects – 'The project manager', came the reply. 'What happens if a customer complains about quality?' – 'We kick the project manager's arse.' When I asked Scicon, a large consultancy group, the same question, their reply was that the managing director was responsible for quality. I asked them to explain, and they said, 'If a project's having trouble meeting its target dates, there's always a temptation to start cutting corners on quality to save time. If you know that any quality problems will be laid at the managing director's door, you think twice before cutting those corners'. That was the problem at the oil company. No one in senior management believed that they had any responsibilities towards quality. It was all down to the project manager.

Going back to the yacht equipment firm, I asked the project manager what he did about quality. I was told that all the firm's staff were 'the best' – in other words, there was no quality planning and only cursory quality inspections until the product was handed over. I asked if there were ever quality problems reported by the customer after handover. 'Oh, yes', came the reply, 'that's another headache I have to handle.' I asked if this ever had an adverse effect on future orders. He nodded and explained how hard he had to work to fix the problem and restore good relations. 'Why', he said, 'I've even sent staff down to the Mediterranean to fix a problem on the spot.' Even after this I could not get him to see that the concept of building in quality and checking as you went along was a good one. 'We don't have time', was his reply. It is an interesting thought that you may not have time to get it right the first time because some of your staff are out correcting the problems caused by getting it wrong the last time. I think that is one 'Which came first, the chicken or the egg?' question that I could answer.

Project quality plans

In my time as Chief Examiner of the PRINCE2 examinations, one of the questions to get the poorest response was, 'Write a project quality plan'. Candidates would write about a project quality plan, discuss the quality path diagram, but very few would actually do what the question asked and write a plan for the project in the examination scenario. It was clear that this was a topic on which training courses did not spend much time, although everyone would agree that it is an important part of project quality thinking. Below is a project quality plan that you can use as a template. I hope it leads to some good project quality plans for your projects. The entries in italics are hints on what kind of entry you should make, and you should replace the notes that are in italics with statements relevant to your own project.

Project quality plan example

Customer's quality expectations

Able to achieve the purpose defined in the product description. Able to meet the quality criteria defined in the product description.

(Extra entries may be made for each type of expectation, e.g. Performance, appearance, maintainability, longevity, level of staff capable of using the product after no more than xx amount of training.)

Acceptance criteria

(See also the acceptance criteria examples given earlier.)

The product passes the tests defined in document *XXX* before handover for customer acceptance testing.

The product passes the customer acceptance tests defined in document *YYY*.

The product is delivered within the time constraints identified in the PID.

The product costs are held within the tolerance boundaries defined in the PID.

Product reliability during customer acceptance testing is twenty-four hours mean time between failure (MTBF) and two hours mean time to repair (MTTR), reducing by the end to zero faults over a seven-day period.

Quality responsibilities

Project manager

The project manager is responsible for the planning and monitoring of all quality work, including work done by customer and supplier staff.

Senior user

The senior user is accountable for the quality of all products delivered by the users, such as the specification of requirements and user acceptance testing. The senior user is also responsible for ensuring that user staff check that the products being delivered by the supplier will meet the specified requirements.

Senior supplier

The senior supplier is accountable for the quality of all products delivered by supplier staff.

Team managers

Team managers are responsible for ensuring that all quality checks defined in the quality log are correctly staffed, implemented and the results posted in the quality log. There must be liaison with project assurance relating to the selection of appropriate quality reviewers and the timing of checks.

Project assurance

As delegated by the relevant project board member, project assurance is responsible for ensuring that appropriate staff are involved in the checking of product quality at selected moments in the product's creation. It is also responsible to the project board for monitoring quality work via entries in the quality log and discussions with those involved in quality inspections. A further responsibility of project assurance is to be involved in the impact analysis of any new project issues, looking for any impact on quality, performance, risks and the business case.

Quality assurance (if you have one)

The (*company's*) quality assurance function is responsible for recommending and providing the standards required for the project, monitoring their use and effectiveness. In order to do this work, QA will take a project assurance role on behalf of (*the senior supplier, senior user or both*).

Standards to be met

PRINCE2 will be used as the project management standard. The specialist work will conform to the standards contained in the supplier's quality management standard (QMS), *e.g. documents will be created using Microsoft Word software version 7.*

Key product quality criteria

What is of key importance to the customer? The customer's quality expectations should hold a clue, e.g. easy to use, reliable, accurate, etc.

The quality control and audit processes to be applied to project management

At the start of the project the project board will agree to the project initiation document on behalf of the business, user and supplier interests. This contains the necessary information, as defined in the PRINCE2 manual, to describe the required products, their quality, the business case for the project, the project plan and the project management controls to be applied.

At the end of each stage the project manager will provide the project board with an end stage report, which will define the performance of the stage against its plan, and reassess the status of the project plan, the business case and risks. The report will also include an assessment of the project management method and its use. The project board will use this in its decision on whether to continue with the project.

At the end of the project the project manager will provide an end project report to the project board. This will compare the success of the project in meeting the requirements defined in the project initiation document, together with any agreed changes.

At close of the project the project manager will provide a lessons learned report to the project board for onward transmission to the quality assurance *(or project management support)* department. This will document the good and bad lessons learned during the use of the project management methods, techniques and tools.

Those with project assurance responsibility will have the opportunity to comment on each of these reports.

The quality control and audit processes to be applied to the specialist work

All specialist documents created during the project will be subject to a quality review. Depending on the decision of the project manager and those holding project assurance responsibility, the quality review may be formal or informal.

> Specialist products *(what type?)* will be subject to *(whatever method of test is suitable)*.
>
> Is there a specific role for the site's quality assurance function?

Change management procedures

Have you got a company standard for change control? If so, refer to where it can be found. If not, then:

> The project will use the change control procedure in the PRINCE2 manual. All requests for change, off-specifications and questions will be raised as project issues, logged, have their impact assessed and decisions made about them by the appointed change authority. *XXXX* will be responsible for the administration of the change control procedure.

Configuration management plan

All specialist and management products will be subjected to version control. All products that are part of the project will carry the prefix *PPP*. Specialist products will have a second prefix of 'S' and management products will carry a secondary prefix of 'M'. Products will have a unique four-digit number. The version number will be VV.DD, where VV indicates a version and DD indicates versions of this. The first draft of a product will always be version 0.01. Thus the total identifier for a product will be:

PPPSXXXX.VV.DD *(This section can be replaced with a reference to the use of a standard configuration management method that has been agreed between customer and supplier.)*

XXXX will be responsible for the administration of the configuration management method.

Tools to be used

Enter here any quality tools or configuration management software to be used. For example, use of the version facility in Microsoft Word, a spell checker or word count. Any other quality tools that relate to the type of product, e.g. stress testers, soak testing equipment for computer boards, bounce equipment for car suspensions, crash rigs etc.

Quality review

The quality log

Many people have only a vague idea of what the quality log's purpose is. They can tell you where it is created and often that the project manager will enter details of planned quality checks in it. But then it comes to a full stop. The real purpose of the quality log is for team managers or individuals to enter the results of each quality check in it. This enables the project manager and project assurance to ensure that the checks are being done – a Gantt chart often does not tell you this – whose work it is, what the results are and whether the product has now passed the quality checks. If you have been around project management long enough, you will know that there may be a world of difference between being told that a product is 'finished' and that product receiving approval of those who will use it. The quality log provides this information and can be used

to identify any resources having trouble delivering a quality product. When an examination question asks about communication between teams and the project manager, many forget the use of the updated quality log.

Risk

We need to start looking for risks even before we ask the project board for permission to enter the initiation stage. What is the point of wasting time and money on a project where the risks outweigh the benefits? There may be risks inherent in the project mandate. It may be based on out-of-date information, unchecked assumptions, and may be vague in what is required.

I remember one IT project for the government. The project had to start in order to meet the government's target end date, no decision on which agency would 'own' the project had been made (there were two possibilities, and neither wanted the job), and it was clear that legislation to define the product would still be passing through Parliament over the next several months.

The project mandate might state a target date that is clearly impossible, given the features that the final product should have. There are many other risks that might be evident in the SU process, for example, the given project approach may be at odds with the customer's quality expectations, or may be an approach that will create the risk of not completing the project on time.

Once the project plan and business case have been refined, these may change current risks (for better or worse) or create new ones. What about risks that some of the benefits are not achievable, or that lack of information about the current state of things means that measuring benefits after delivering the product may be impossible?

A colleague (thanks, Craig) quoted me the following approach to risk in an organization where he had worked: 'Due to the tight timescales of xxx project, it is deemed futile to employ a risk management strategy.' I think they had a risk strategy all right – and a risky one at that! I can just see the owners of the *Titanic* saying that on the first crossing.

Change control

If you do not control change, then you do not control the project. Many years ago I took over my first project from someone who had moved on to a new company. The project had dragged on way past its profitability, and as it was a fixed price project I wanted to know what had happened. I discovered that the customer had been responsible for the design. When it came to us, the team discovered that the design was based on a technical impossibility. The design was sent back and the whole team twiddled their thumbs for a month until it was corrected. No project issue was raised, no impact analysis, the target date had not been renegotiated and the customer was not charged a single penny extra. There were some other later changes completely ignored by the project manager in terms of cost and time, but that was the big one.

Here is another salutary tale about change control, but this time about a consultancy company that used it to its advantage. The company would watch for invitations to tender that were vague in their statement of requirements. They would bid low to ensure that they got the work, then work their way through the project, saying, 'Ah, but that was not clear in your specification'. A project issue would be raised – a request for change, naturally – and the customer was faced with a never-ending avalanche of requests for extra time and money to implement these 'changes'. I was told that they used this in some projects to treble the original quote.

Setting tolerances

Tolerances follow the PRINCE2 four layers of management. Senior management set project tolerances for the project board. The project board sets stage tolerances for the project manager, and the project manager sets tolerances for team managers (part of a work package). If there is a threat to those tolerances, the situation is escalated to the level of management that set those tolerances. That is, if work package tolerances come under threat, this is escalated to the project manager. If stage tolerances are threatened, the project manager escalates to the project board, and if project tolerances are threatened, the project board executive must escalate to senior management. Tolerance is a key part of management by exception – 'get on with the job unless these parameters are threatened'.

In the PRINCE2 manual tolerance has been extended to cover more things than just:

time, e.g. ±10 per cent of the project plan, ± ten days, or 'must be finished by 15 October'

cost, e.g. ±5 per cent of the project plan, ±£10 000, or 'the cost limit is £250 000'

scope, e.g. 'Yes, you can have the house by that date, but the garage won't be finished'

quality, e.g. 'You can have the car in any colour you like, as long as it's black'.

Tolerance now covers:

- *risk*, e.g. how much risk is the project board prepared to take to achieve the final product? Risk tolerance can also be used to look at the other tolerances (cost, time, quality, benefits and resources/people). For example, if you were to ask a burglar what his/her risk tolerance was, would it relate to the financial gain to be made or just the risk of getting caught? Moving into the field of industry, what is the risk tolerance of not using a machine's safeguards? A time saving (or laziness or poor maintenance) versus a large fine if caught or an expensive court case if sued by an employee who gets hurt.
- *benefit*, e.g. 'as long as we get at least 5 per cent increase in business from the project' or 'I'm hoping for £1000 profit, but I'm prepared to settle for £500'.

The cost and time of a requested change should not be confused with tolerance. Tolerance is there because planning is not an exact science. You are planning a part of the future, using resources whose performance levels you may not know in a possibly strange environment. Tolerance is not an allowance set aside to pay for 'small' changes that the user wants. That is called a change budget, and is a separate pot of money agreed with the executive during initiation and set aside to pay for change requests.

Refining the business case and risks

Investment appraisal

By the time that you reach sub-process IP3, you have created a project quality plan and the project plan. Both of these contain information that may change the outline business case and risks that you quoted in the project brief. Quality may cost more to build into the product and verify than you had estimated. The more detailed project plan may reveal extra time and cost requirements than you (or the original feasibility study) thought. There may be risks in failing to achieve the required quality. The project plan may contain risks or change those risks that you listed during creation of the project brief. The situation for both may have got better – but, knowing projects as we do, both will have got worse!

Setting up project files

Not many of us enjoy filing, so not many of us like to spend time thinking about a filing system. The PRINCE2 method offers one. Why not use it? Or use it as a basis for developing your own?

The filing system must be done in conjunction with the configuration management plan. This is a good time to check that you have made adequate plans for project support.

Compiling the project initiation document

Much of what goes into the project initiation document has (or should have) been seen by the project board before, e.g. the project objectives, the project management team structure may not have changed since 'authorizing initiation'. But initiation gives us the chance to revisit these things, and expand and clarify them. We may not have made decisions on the use of team managers during our earlier team design time; the project plan is new and may have revealed a lot more information for our risk log. The business case will have been expanded, we will have made decisions on controls and created a communication plan.

It is a fallacy that senior management are impressed by huge documents. They probably do not have time to read them. Keep the project initiation document as slim as possible. Put in a diagram of the project management team, but say that individual job descriptions are filed and can be inspected if wished. Put in a Gantt chart or product checklist, but do not put in the product breakdown structure, the product flow diagram or the product descriptions.

I have to include this conversation between Craig Kilford and a project manager, whose project was slipping. My thanks to Craig for passing it on.

> *Craig*: 'Okay, Tony, we need to raise an exception report, because we said at the start of the project that we have one month's tolerance on time for this project, and after looking at the plan, you seem to have slipped'.
> *Tony*: 'Okay, so this means another bureaucratic form does it?'
> *Craig*: 'What do you mean by bureaucratic?'

> *Tony*: 'Well, this PRINCE2, it makes you do stuff that you never use.'
>
> *Craig*: 'Does it? What documents have you created in PRINCE2 and not used?'
>
> *Tony*: 'Well, for one the project plan. We spent the time creating it at the start and haven't even looked at it since then!'
>
> *Craig*: 'Ah.'

This came to me through the PRINCE2 forum, PRINCE2Projects@Yahoogroups.com. It was followed by some correspondence from others, one of whom even agreed with Tony that the project plan was a pretty useless document. I felt moved to ask how he got the project cost for entry into the business case, and against what did the project board check progress at each end stage assessment?

Another quote from Craig Kilford is a direct extract from a section in an agreed project initiation document that he saw:

> 6) Project Plan
> To be completed at a later date.

Levels of plan

Many people think that the project plan is the only mandatory plan in PRINCE2. This is not correct. Stage plans are also mandatory. You have only to read the various parts of the manual to realize that this must be so. In 'managing stage boundaries' you create the next stage plan. In sub-process DP3, 'authorizing a stage', the project board has to approve a stage plan. The manual clearly states that a stage plan is created immediately before that stage. So, every stage needs a plan, the project board must approve each stage plan, and a stage plan is only developed as the previous stage is finishing. From where did the confusion come?

If it is a small project with only one specialist stage – i.e. the project has two stages, initiation and the remainder of the project – the project manager may choose to combine the stage plan for the remainder of the project in the project plan. In such a case, we may physically have only a project plan, but it includes a stage plan.

Team plans

Many people blindly accept the statement that team plans are created in sub-process MP1, 'accepting a work package', without connecting this to another statement that a stage plan is created in sub-process SB1, 'planning a stage'. If we think about it, it is fairly clear that team plans will have an impact on a stage plan, and it is not a great deal of use presenting a stage plan to the project board until you have agreed the team plans that may form a big part of that stage plan. So although the two sub-processes do not appear to be connected in the manual, agreeing team plans will have to be part of preparing a stage plan, certainly for any major work to be done by teams.

What is a plan?

This question takes me back to the project manager in the small yacht equipment firm. I asked him to show me a typical set of plans for one of his projects and his overall plan showing all projects and the allocation of staff across the projects. What he showed me looked something like that in Table 4.

I am sure that my fading memory has caused me to invent the odd word or two, but this is basically it – no further detail of how many days in those months, no statement of how many staff involved, nothing. I asked to see the more detailed plan, only to be told that this was it! Nor was there a plan showing all the projects, no resource utilization detail and no cost information. The plan was never updated with any actual progress figures. I do not know how it worked for him as a plan. I only know that he had nothing to show him the status of anything. If he wanted to know, he had to go and ask the staff working on the project.

Table 4 Projects and staff plan.

2 hatches for mv 'Swanney Whistle'

	Jan	Feb	March	April
Measure	X			
Design		X		
Build			X	
Fit				X

Writing a product description

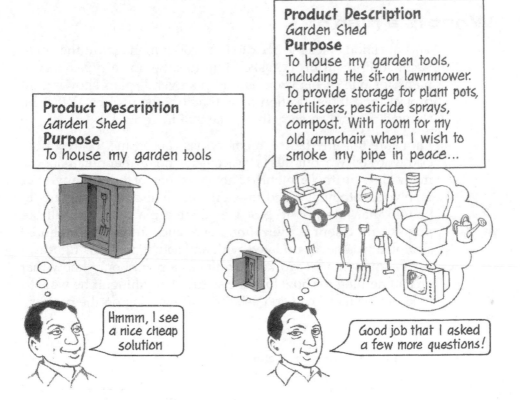

Many people have difficulty in writing good quality criteria. Many of them are bland or immeasurable. Here is a list of quality criteria that can be applied to almost any document.

Dooument quallty criteria

Documents should have the following attributes:

- Be clear and concise.
- Be accurate.
- Be comprehensive.
- The grammar and spelling are correct.
- The product meets the defined standard.
- The product is on the required form.
- Reflect accurately the information contained in/required by the derivation material.
- The information is at the correct level for the readership.
- Be free from jargon which is unknown or unexplained to the readership.
- Information is provided under every expected heading.
- The information provided under each heading is appropriate to that heading.
- Input has been provided from all the relevant parties.
- The document's summary/conclusions are consistent with the body of the report.
- The product fulfils its stated purpose.
- Be delivered on time.
- The contents match the contents page.
- The product's author is clearly indicated.
- The distribution list is provided and correct.

There are many methods of estimating. Some of these differ quite radically according to the area of work, so PRINCE2 does not attempt to cover many specifics about estimating. But there are a few general words of advice that might be useful.

I remember a project manager telling me that he always thought that he had a good plan, but by the end of the first week he had to work overtime to keep to it. We looked at his plan, and he had scheduled himself 100 per cent on the key technical work of the project. When I asked where the time was for him to write reports and update the plan, there was the answer – his overtime.

Most planning tools allow you to give a percentage availability for each resource. Even on a small project a project manager should not make him/herself available for technical work more than 50 per cent of the time. Once you have a team of five or six, you should not be doing any of the technical work, just project managing.

An early part of estimating that in PRINCE2 you would do in the process PL1, 'designing a plan', is to identify what parameters you will use in estimation. What percentage availability will you give to each resource? Who needs allowance for telephone calls, ad hoc meetings, giving advice? Do you need to make allowances for learning curves for some resources? Do you have the same efficiency ratings for experienced, semi-experienced and trainee resources? Do you make manual adjustments for these as you estimate each task, or do you put the adjustments in the parameters for each resource and let the software make the necessary calculations? In longer projects how do you cope with holidays, sick leave and training? Do you wait until they happen and then adjust your plans or do you forecast when they are likely to occur and build the time into your plans, so any adjustment does not seriously affect your ability to hit planned target dates?

Creating a work package

Work packages are wonderful things if used sensibly. Linked with product descriptions they can spell out an agreement for a piece of work clearly and easily. How many times have you asked someone to do an apparently simple piece of work, only for problems to arise? They did not do everything you wanted, the result was not presented in the way that you wanted, they did not take everything into account, they made assumptions, you had made assumptions, they missed something that you said (or you think you said) – the list is endless. Documenting it against a checklist of headings and discussing it does help improve communications.

Figure 22 shows a form that I put on a postcard and fill in when giving someone a work package.

Product descriptions and work packages can be very powerful things, if used properly. I tried this out on a handyman/gardener who came to do a job for me in the garden. I knew that I would not be around when he started the work, so I wrote a product description for it and embedded this in a work package, which I gave to the gardener. Afterwards, I asked if he had been offended by the formality of the work package, and he said it was good to get clear, unambiguous instructions, rather than vague ones. Inevitably the vague ones had forgotten some things and not made others clear, resulting in extra work when he thought that he had finished.

Here is the work package that I gave him.

WORK PACKAGE								
Date of origin		Date allocated		Allocated to		Interface with	
Work package description								
Products to be produced								
Tools								
Effort		Cost		Start date		Target date	
Constraints								
Risks								
Reporting				Sign-off				

Figure 22 Example of a work package form

Cleaning up the garden

Work package

Date: 20 March 2002

Person authorized: Dougal

Work package description

> Clean up the borders, hedges and patio of 42 The Cuttings, East Cheam and remove the garden refuse created by the work

Product description

Title: Borders, hedges and patio.

Purpose: To be a tidy and attractive surround to the house

Composition

> Weed-free and bramble-free borders
>
> Dead-headed hydrangeas
>
> Pruned roses
>
> Clipped hedges
>
> Borders with dead plants removed
>
> Weed-free and clean patio

Quality criteria

> Meets composition section.
>
> Hedge at side of house cut on a level with the side wall
>
> Front face of hedge to be trimmed back to present a flat, even appearance
>
> All cuttings and rubbish caused by the work removed from the premises
>
> Patio to have any surface dirt, algae and weeds removed
>
> The plant pots on the patio will have to be moved onto the lawn during patio cleaning and replaced afterwards

Quality method: Visual inspection

Tools to be used: You are to provide your own tools. If needed, a power point is available in the house porch

Interfaces to be maintained during the work.

> You do not need permission from my neighbour at number 40 if you have to enter her garden to do any of this work, but if you need to enter the garden of number 44, I will need to get her permission first.

Effort, cost, start and end dates

> We have agreed that you will do the work on Thursday, 21 March 2002. You have estimated the work at four hours at a cost of £5 an hour

Sign-off: I will pay in cash on completion after a satisfactory quality check described below.
Constraints
Avoid entering the grounds of number 44 without first
consulting me. Don't use any weed killers or patio cleaner fluid that may damage the lawn.
Quality checking arrangements: I will check the work against
the product description for the job.

Note that some of the work package headings, such as 'reporting', have been dropped. As with all things it is a matter of
common sense and scaling the contents to the job in question. If
you look at the above information, you could decide whether
you wanted to give it to the gardener as it stands or give only
part of it, or give him the information verbally and keep the
'written' information to yourself as just a checklist that you have
said everything.

Interfaces

A work package has two headings that seem to confuse people,
'interfaces to be satisfied' and 'interfaces to be maintained'. The
first is about the interfaces that the product you are creating will
have when it is in operational use. For example, 'that new
fountain pen that you are designing must be capable of fitting
any of our standard range of pen nibs', or 'the newsletter is to be
read by all levels of staff'.

'Interfaces to be maintained' is about with whom the team (or
recipient of the work package) has to liaise or work in creating
or procuring the product.

How do you assess progress? I have seen many projects where this was done from time sheets, but I still have not seen one that was successful. I have, however, seen project team members staring vacantly at the ceiling on a Friday afternoon, desperately trying to remember what they have done during the week and how long it took them. At a certain distillery time sheets were not only used to update the stage plans, they were input to the payroll department as a record of the hours worked (and to be paid). Time had to be recorded in multiples of seven and a half minutes – do not ask me why! Result – making the time sheet add up to 37.5 hours was the first target. Work on the various tasks was fudged in order to arrive at the correct total. In terms of accurate plan updates, it was a joke. Why do it? Are you really using time sheets to check on the accuracy of your estimates? I know the theory of this, but in all my years I have not seen this done. I have seen time sheets used to update plans with the amount of time spent, but it is that old saying, 'Garbage in, garbage out'. It is worth setting down what information you want back from the project staff. When did you start the task? Have you finished it? If not, will you finish it on a different day to that shown in the plan? In most cases you do not need – or use – any more than this, and the less information you require, the more you are likely to get the truth.

Another question for you – how much time have you allowed in your stage or team plan to update the plan?

Highlight report

Someone once said to me, 'Don't write a progress report for a busy manager that takes longer to read than the time between his/her phone calls – and that is one page'. The longer it gets, the less likely it is to be read. If you have something important to say, say it in the first few lines. A librarian once said to me, 'If people are not hooked by the time they have read the first paragraph on the first page of a book, it's back on the shelf'. Telling people that major jobs have started may be OK, but it does not compare to telling them what has been finished, and saying that a job is x per cent complete is just a waste of time and paper. Tell them what has been delivered and what will be delivered by the time of the next report. If you said in the last report that something would be finished and it is not, that needs stating in a problem section, together with why and a statement that it will be finished before the next report. Tell them where the stage stands with regard to the planned budget and time, including tolerances. Add any other potential problems that the project board should know about and you have said all the important stuff.

Not many project boards want a huge report, even at the end of a stage. Ask the project board members in advance if they want more than is suggested in the composition section of the product description for the report. Do not write an essay if they are happy with bullet points.

Gateways or gate reviews

These are not PRINCE2 terms. As PRINCE2 is owned by the OGC, a section of the Treasury, the PRINCE2 manual has to acknowledge some parallel terms used in government and other circles. A gate review is described as 'a point at the end of a stage or phase where a decision is made on whether to continue with the project'. The difference between this and a PRINCE2 end stage assessment is that people outside the project are asked to participate. These are usually experts; consultants, auditors or people with a specialist knowledge of the subject area. From reports that I have had, the addition of such people can be a help. Just because it is a term used in government does not have to mean 'bureaucracy'. One PRINCE2 Practitioner who took part in a Gateway 4 review said the following:

> I have just participated in a readiness for service gateway review as an interviewee, so the following general observations might be helpful:
>
> The review is a fast, tight process conducted by a specialist team appointed by OGC. One consultant and one person with specialist knowledge of the subject area interviewed me. The total time for the review is less than 1 week, and leads to a report to the senior responsible officer (SRO – another government term for executive) indicating what areas of risk arise from the current status of the project. The SRO is then free to act upon the report as they deem fit.
>
> This is not a substitute for the PRINCE methodology. The reviewers were very conscious of the PRINCE2 controls and were looking to see what evidence of overall project readiness they could draw from them. Good evidence derived from use of the methodology is likely to assist them greatly in their job.
>
> Given the limited time the team have, they cannot be expected to trawl through the documentation looking for scattered evidence of control, component and process conformance. It is important to be able to present this to the team ready for their review.

On taking over from another project manager

This can be a chance to sail to glory on the back of someone else's hard work – but more often than not, it is a poisoned chalice. As in buying a second-hand car, believe nothing that the outgoing project manager tells you about the superb condition in which he/she is leaving the project unless you have seen it, heard it from at least seven independent witnesses and hold a high court order confirming your predecessor as a registered saint. The executive may be shedding a tear, but is it really because your predecessor is going?

Here is a little checklist if you happen to find yourself in this position:

Project initiation document

1. Confirm that a documented and agreed project brief exists.
2. Is there an approved project initiation document?
3. Does the project initiation document contain all the expected information?

Business case

4. Was a genuine business case created?
5. Are the measurements realistic?
6. Is the business case being maintained?
7. Is it examined at the correct points?

Risks

8. Does a risk log exist?
9. Is it up to date?
10. Are there owners for all risks?
11. Do stage/team plans reflect the necessary risk planning, resources, monitoring and controlling activities?
12. When was the status of risk log entries last checked?
13. Should the risk estimates be reviewed?

Plans

14. At what point in the project are you joining?
15. Check that a project plan exists and is up to date.
16. Confirm that there is an up-to-date current stage plan.
17. What is the status of actual budget and schedule figures against the project and current stage plans?
18. What are the agreed tolerance levels for the project and stage plans? Do these seem realistic?
19. Are there any detailed plans covering the future activities of the project? If so, are these:
    (a) realistic
    (b) agreed by those who will do the work
    (c) approved by the project board?

Organization

20. Is there a project board? Does it function properly?
21. Confirm that all tasks and responsibilities in the organization roles have been allocated and agreed.
22. Confirm that the organization roles are being carried out as agreed and that no gaps exist.
23. Meet with all project board members and judge their attitude to the project.
24. Confirm who is carrying out the assurance roles.
25. Check on their availability to the project – planned and actual.
26. What are the assurance role descriptions? Do these cover all your requirements? What is their attitude? To what organization structure do they belong outside the project? Where do their loyalties lie?
27. Do team members have up-to-date work packages?
28. Have completed work packages been assessed for performance and filed?
29. Has the outgoing project manager provided an assessment of each team member?

Quality

30. Is there a quality file? Is it up to date?
31. Are quality reviews being carried out?
32. Do the assurance roles have the opportunity to select which reviews they attend? Does this include the user and supplier assurance roles?
33. Are you satisfied with the number of quality reviews attended by the assurance roles?
34. Is the quality review procedure being followed?
35. Is there a satisfactory quality plan at both project and stage level?

Project issues

36. Check the logging of all project issues.
37. Are project issues being assessed for their impact on risks and the business case?
38. Is the project issue procedure being carried out fully and correctly?
39. What is the current status of all open project issues?

40. Is all extra work caused by approved project issues being correctly approved?
41. Have stage plans reflected this extra work?

Configuration management

42. Have a product status account produced for you.
43. Check the product status account against the actuals of the stage plan to see if they agree on the status of products.
44. Have a configuration audit done.

Controls

45. Does a communication plan exist? Is it being followed?
46. How often are highlight reports being sent to the project board? When was the last one sent?
47. Is the project board happy with the highlight report content?
48. Are checkpoint reports coming in with sufficient regularity to provide highlight report input?
49. Are the checkpoint reports accurately depicting the real state of the stage and any team plans?

At the back of the PRINCE2 manual there is a project health check. Why not suggest that the project you are to take over is put through a health check?

End project report

Some people have said to me that they do not see the difference between the end project report and the lessons learned report. I can understand this; the manual has not been very clear about the difference in the past.

First, they are for different audiences. The end project report is for the project board. The lessons learned report is for those looking after standards. The end project report says to the project board, 'This is how I have performed against the project initiation document that we agreed, plus or minus any changes that you have agreed since then. Have I delivered everything that you wanted? How did I perform against the time, cost and quality parameters?'

The lessons learned report looks at the use of the project management standards, and comments on whether the standards were obeyed, whether they did the job they were supposed to do and whether any standards were weak or missing. It does the same job for any specialist tools or techniques used.

This is not just for project issues that the project board decided
to defer. Are there any risks that will still exist into the product's
operational life? If the project was prematurely closed, are there
any finished, intermediate or unfinished products that can be used
elsewhere, should be preserved or are in need of security, health
or safety measures, e.g. an unfinished piece of construction?

I do not know why people have problems putting one of these together. I suppose one of the major problems is not writing lessons down in the lessons learned log as they occur, but waiting until the end of the project before trying to remember them.

It seems pretty simple. It has two sections, project management and specialist. In each section there are headings for what processes, tools or standards worked well, which went badly and which would have been useful had they been available. I know the product outline in the manual has a few more suggestions, but these are the key entries.

Here is an example of what might go in a lessons learned report. Again tailor anything in italics to your own projects. The other text should be acceptable for everyone.

Example lessons learned report

Purpose

The purpose of this lessons learned report is to pass on to other projects the useful lessons that have been learned from this project.

The central support office (CSO), which is responsible for the site *quality management system*, should use the data in the report to refine, change and improve project management standards and its training.

Project management

What went well?

The use of product-based planning went well, especially in the planning workshops held with service delivery and the users. The planning process was easily understood, even by those completely new to planning of any kind. The involvement of service delivery at the planning stage of the project greatly improved their understanding and participation, and contributed to much better co-operation between the development team and service delivery than has been the case in past projects.

The workshop to produce a project initiation document worked very well. It had a number of benefits:

Taking the team off-site to a hotel was very cost- and time-effective. The project initiation document was produced in two and a half days, whereas other projects of a similar size have taken several weeks.

Bringing together the team that represented developer, user and service delivery to create the project initiation document created an excellent team spirit that lasted throughout the project. This is not the company's normal experience.

The workshop's second objective was to give an overview of the project management method to those of the team unfamiliar with it. Apart from achieving the training objectives, this gave background and understanding of what the team was trying to achieve with the project initiation document's creation.

The appointment and use of the project board contributed greatly to the success of the project. There was much more ownership by the project board than from senior management on projects not run under PRINCE2.

What went badly?

The product descriptions produced originally were very bland and therefore virtually useless, particularly the quality criteria. A special exercise, using a PRINCE2 consultant had to be undertaken. The new product descriptions were much better (see above section).

There were some early problems with the quality review technique. Some users failed to turn up as planned. Some of these sent a late apology; others forgot or said they were too busy when asked why they were absent. None sent in question lists. Another problem was reviewers turning up who had clearly not read the product in advance. This caused delays and meant that the review could not be run according to the established procedure. Eventually these problems were sorted out through action from the project board, but much more 'progress chasing' to get question lists submitted in advance had to be done. The attempt to use earned value analysis (EVA) was not a success. Many mistakes in the figures were made by the CSO through lack of training. The results, even when corrected, and the specific EVA jargon did not seem to be understood by the project board, again through a lack of training.

The insistence by the project board on monthly progress meetings was not very useful and these were stopped after three months.

Project management aspects lacking

The lack of a recognized document structure and approach to the production of the business case caused unnecessary work. The idea of using the feasibility study business case did not work. It did not contain benefit measurements that could be applied in any post-project review.

Technique assessment

Product-based planning was, apart from the problem with product descriptions mentioned under 'what went badly', very helpful. It eased the planning process and assisted in communication with the users. It also provided the right basis for earned value analysis (but see the problems that we had with that under the 'what went badly?' heading).

Support tool assessment

The use of PMW was in the main very successful. The ability to consolidate the team plans at stage and project levels saved a great deal of planning and reporting time. The network planning part of the tool fitted in very well with the product flow diagrams produced.

Problems were encountered in using the automatic scheduling feature. This must be used with care and users must be very disciplined in filing the plan before using this feature.

The PMW ability to create time sheets for individual progress reporting saved the project support function much time.

Abnormal events which affected operation of the project management method

The public announcement of an implementation date before the project plan had been produced had a serious effect on the project. When the project plan was produced, it was obvious that not everything could be delivered by the published date. The project was pushed into an unnecessary exercise of de-scoping that was expensive and time-consuming because of the many project and product interdependencies that the project has.

Project issue analysis

After some teething problems with users who were not accustomed to the procedure the project issue procedure worked very well. A breakdown of the project issues received and actions taken is given in the end project report.

Of the thirty-three change requests received, eight concerned functions that were known before the project and should have been part of the user specification.

Whilst the volume of project issues was not great, they did require considerable time to decide on the course of action, mainly due to the busy work schedule of the project board members.

Recommendations

More and better training in the writing of product descriptions must be undertaken in order to make these useful products and not be seen as a bureaucratic waste of time. It would be worth our while to train up at least two people from CSO as experts in writing product descriptions. In the medium and long term this is a more effective and cost-conscious solution than continuing to use a PRINCE2 consultant. (It should be said, however, that great value was gained by using the particular PRINCE2 consultant obtained for this work in this project, and it would be sensible to ask this consultant to undertake the training.)

Training in the quality review process should be given to all who may have to participate in these in a project.

The company should adopt a standard way of producing and documenting the business case. We should either work to the product description given in the PRINCE2 manual, or get our finance department to create one for us.

If EVA is to be used, all concerned with creating and using the figures must be trained in the technique.

The use of a software package for the production of planning networks, Gantt charts and time sheets should be extended to all projects. A separate project should assess our needs in this area and recommend a standard tool to be used.

Consideration should be given to the setting aside of a change budget and a change authority below the level of the project board for future projects to avoid having to go back to the project board for finance to cover required minor changes. This project was not a particularly volatile one in terms of user requirements. It was still difficult to get project board consensus on the implementation of change requests. Future projects should consider very carefully whether decisions (within constraints) on changes could be handed down to a lower level, e.g. a change authority. If project assurance responsibilities are delegated, those appointed could form the members of this change authority.

Post-project review plan

After how many projects do people actually check to see if the expected benefits were gained? The vast majority of projects do not have a business case with measurable figures of their expectations. Of those that have, many are never checked after the product has been delivered. Often this only happens when the project has been a disaster and management are looking at the points of failure.

The post-project review plan may not be a plan as we know it, Jim lad. It may not be delivered by the project manager in the form of a Gantt chart. Its purpose is to offer a clearer idea to the executive of:

- when the checks for the achievement of benefits can begin
- how achievement can be measured
- what resources will be needed.

Achievement of benefits may not be measurable for weeks or months after a product has begun its operational life. Consider the Channel Tunnel. Over what period of time do you think its achievement of benefits should be measured? The post-project review plan may have to suggest more than one point in the product's use when measurements should be taken.

Measurement will usually depend on the measurements, taken before the project began, of the situation that existed without the product. But what tools will be needed, what will have to be measured? Is it straightforward? How much extra cash has it generated or are there other measurements, such as customer satisfaction, maintenance costs, staff required, staff morale?

What skills will be needed in order to carry out the review? Remember, the PRINCE2 philosophy is that the project has finished, the project manager will have moved on to other work, and responsibility for the post-project review belongs to the executive. The executive is unlikely to do the review personally, although retaining responsibility, so what kind of skills and how many people is the review going to need?

Apart from a straight match against the business case, there are normally other headings to the post-project review. It may need to check the users' reaction to the product. Are there comments or grumbles that should be turned into maintenance projects to improve the product? Has the new product caused a bottleneck farther down the production line? Has the new product had an adverse effect on other company products? Has the new product produced some unexpected benefits? Has the world changed since the project began, and the environment in which the product sits is now better or worse for the success of that product?

When looking for the skills and resources to carry out the review, it is often useful and possible to involve those who took project assurance roles in the project. They have the background knowledge and experience of the environment.

Part III

Managing small projects

How small a job or project does it have to be before I stop trying to apply PRINCE2 to it? When does PRINCE2 become a bureaucratic overkill? How do I control a job that is too small to be called a project? How do I control a project that needs more than one person? In this part we look at scaling down PRINCE2 for small projects.

Chapter 1 explores the use of work packages for very small projects. The idea here is that often some jobs can seem so small that it would be ridiculous to treat them as projects, yet they often go wrong because we forget to apply basic project discipline to them.

Chapter 2 looks at the bare minimum of PRINCE2 that can be used in smaller projects while still retaining the key features, particularly in the area of control.

Chapter 3's approach is to use a matrix, where you can balance certain of your prospective project's characteristics against the scope of the PRINCE2 elements that you should use. In this context, a 'small' project would still be one requiring several staff.

Chapter 4 looks at a reduced core of PRINCE2 processes and management products that can be used for smaller projects while still retaining the essential PRINCE2 concepts. Its four processes are fixed, unlike the matrix in Chapter 3, but everything in them is scaled down to easily manageable proportions. It is a method used very successfully by Tesco stores. Again the project may be small, but would still be big enough to use stages, each of which would need some kind of approval – formal or informal.

Chapter 5 takes each part of the PRINCE2 method and considers the need for it in a small project.

Chapter 6 is a copy of an article written by staff and consultants at Government Communications Headquarters (GCHQ). It is useful in the context of this book because it deals with two problems: how to avoid 'locking up' staff in a project where they are not required full time and it provides an answer to the often difficult relationship between project and line management.

Chapter 7 offers some final reflections on where the thoughts in the section have wandered and tries to summarize the suggestions and look at where the different ideas might apply.

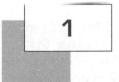

1

How to manage *really* small projects, or 'Honey, I've shrunk the project'

The ideal introduction to project management, I believe, is to start at the bottom, managing a job that requires either just your effort or your giving work instructions to one other person.

Below even a small project there are many stand-alone jobs to be done that can go wrong if we do not set them up correctly. There comes a time (or size of a piece of work to be done) when common sense tells you that you should not dive into creating a project management team for it or consider breaking the work into stages. Let us take a few examples.

- An odd-job gardener is coming to clean up your garden, a job probably taking no more than a day.
- You want your bathroom or kitchen renovated.
- You want someone to write an article for your newsletter.
- You want someone to organize an event at your local golf club.

To coin a phrase from total quality management (TQM), you want to get it right first time. How many times do we hear, or utter ourselves, 'But you didn't say that' or 'Well, why didn't you tell me that' or 'It's a bit late to tell me that now'. So making our total requirements known in a clear and unambiguous way is still needed, however small the work may be.

We also need to advise the person doing the work of any particular tools to use, any constraints, what the target date or time is, how much we expect to pay, anyone else whose input is needed, what to do in case of any problems, etc. Do all of these things sound familiar? Yes, they are exactly the information that we would put in a PRINCE2 work package, and I am suggesting to you that the work package concept can be used for these small, one-off jobs, first to give ourselves a checklist to ensure that we are providing all the information needed, and secondly to provide a clear set of work instructions for the person doing the job.

Let us remind ourselves of what the PRINCE2 manual says about the approach, structure and content of a work package.

Work package

This product will vary in content – and, indeed, in degree of formality – depending on circumstances.

Where the work is being conducted by an individual or a team working directly under the project manager, the work package may be an oral instruction, although there are good reasons for putting it in writing, such as avoidance of misunderstanding and providing a link to performance assessment. Where the work is being carried out by a supplier under a contract and the project manager is part of the customer organization, there is a need for a formal written instruction in line with standards laid down in that contract.

Although the content may vary greatly according to the relationship between the project manager and the recipient of the work package, it should cover:

- *Date* – the date of the agreement between the project manager and the team manager/person authorized.
- *Team or person authorized* – the name of the team manager or individual with whom the agreement has been made.
- *Work package description* – a description of the work to be done.
- *Product description(s)* – this would normally be an attachment of the product description(s) for the products identified in the work package.
- *Techniques/processes/procedures to be used* – any techniques, tools, standards, processes or procedures to be used in the creation of the business products (not including PRINCE2 processes) – including who provides these things.
- *Interfaces to be satisfied by the completed product(s)* – identification of any business products with which the product(s) in the work package will have to interface during their operational life. These may be other products to be produced

by the project, existing products or those to be produced by other projects. An example might be, 'the trailer that you are building must attach to the tow bar at the rear of my car'.

- *Interfaces to be maintained during the work* – with whom must interfaces be maintained while doing the work? These may be people providing information or those who need to receive information.
- *Configuration management requirements* – this will identify any arrangements that must be made by the developer for version control of the products in the work package, obtaining copies of other products or their product descriptions, submission of the product to configuration management, and any need to advise the configuration librarian of changes in the status of the work package products.
- *Stage plan extract* – this will be the relevant section of either the stage plan or product checklist or a pointer to it.
- *Joint agreement on effort, cost, start and end dates, and tolerances* – details of the amounts and dates agreed, plus any tolerances for the work package.
- *Any constraints to be observed* – any constraints (apart from the tolerances) on the work, people to be involved, timings, charges, rules to be followed (for example, security and safety), etc.
- *Reporting arrangements* – the expected frequency and content of checkpoint reports (for a very small work package this may not be needed at all).
- *Problem handling and escalation* – this will normally refer to the procedure for raising project issues and details of any new or changed risks.
- *Sign-off requirements* – the person, role or group who will approve the finished work package products – often yourself.
- *How completion is to be advised* – this will say how the project manager (or person allocating the work package) is to be advised of completion of the work package.

Note that one part of the work package should be a product description. This is still vital in identifying the quality criteria (how you will judge whether the job comes up to scratch), sources of information or products and other useful information. Once you have the format of the work package (or checklist, if you prefer to think of it as that) clear, you can decide whether to make it a formal document with headings, a handwritten note or an oral communication, but remember the advantages of a written document over a verbal communication – 'You didn't ask for that', 'Oh yes I did', 'Oh no you didn't', and so on ad nauseam.

Let us go back to the first of our examples and follow it through, using the idea of creating a work package.

Work package for cleaning up the garden

Date: 20 March 2002

Person authorized: Dougal

Work package description

Clean up the borders, hedges and patio of 42 The Cuttings, East Cheam and remove the garden rubbish created by the work.

Product description

Title: Cleaned borders, hedges and patio.

Purpose: To be a tidy and attractive surround to the house.

Composition:

Weed-free and bramble-free borders.
Dead-headed hydrangeas.
Pruned roses.
Clipped hedges.
Borders with dead plants removed.
Weed-free and clean patio.

Quality criteria:

Meets the Composition section. Hedge at side of house cut on a level with the side wall. Front face of hedge to be trimmed back to present a flat, even appearance. All cuttings and rubbish caused by the work removed from the premises. Patio to have any surface dirt, algae and weeds removed. The plant pots on the patio will have to be moved onto the lawn during patio cleaning and put back afterwards.

Quality method:

Visual inspection against the product description.

Quality checking skills:

I will be responsible for the quality check.

(End of product description)

Tools to be used:

You are to provide your own tools. If needed, a power point is available in the house porch.

Interfaces to be maintained during the work:

You do not need permission from my neighbour at number 40 if you have to enter her garden to do any of this work, but if you need to enter the garden of number 44, I will need to get her permission first.

Effort, cost, start and end dates:

We have agreed that you will do the work on Thursday, 21 March 2002. You have estimated the work at eight hours at a cost of £5 an hour.

Sign-off:

I will agree completion after a satisfactory quality check.

Constraints:

Avoid entering the grounds of number 44 without first consulting me. Do not use any weed killers or patio cleaner fluid that may damage the lawn.

Note that some of the 'normal' work package headings have been dropped, such as 'reporting'. As with all things it is a matter of common sense and scaling the contents to the job in question. If you look at the above information, you can decide whether you want to give it to the gardener as it stands, give him only part of it or tell him the information and keep the 'written' information to yourself as a checklist that you have said everything.

The main point is, does this give you a way of allocating a small job to someone that avoids any confusion on what exactly you want doing, scopes the job and defines the quality you are expecting? If the boot is on the other foot, and someone is giving the small job to you, why not either ask them to complete a work package or at least check the instructions you are given against those expected in a work package and product description?

It may also be worth your while doing a quick product-based plan in your head (or on a piece of paper) to think of such things as sequence and dependencies. On many occasions in the past, I know that I have gone to do a small job, only to realize that I have forgotten some tool that I needed (or my glasses!), or that I have done work packages in the wrong order and need to undo something. Is it also worth considering if there are any risks associated with doing the job? Planning and risk management may be components in a large project management method reference manual, but they also relate to our everyday work.

Figures 23 and 24 are product breakdown structure and product flow diagrams respectively, that you might have created in your mind or on paper if you were to implement the work package.

The PFD shows that after Assembled Tools the next four products could be done in any sequence. If one or more extra resources were available, up to all four could be done at the same time. The flow suggests that these four products would be in place before the cuttings and clippings were removed, i.e. make all the mess, then one clean-up. Again the flow shows that the plant pots can be removed at any time before the patio is cleaned. After the replacement of the plant pots, both diagrams suggest that there would be a final check by the person doing

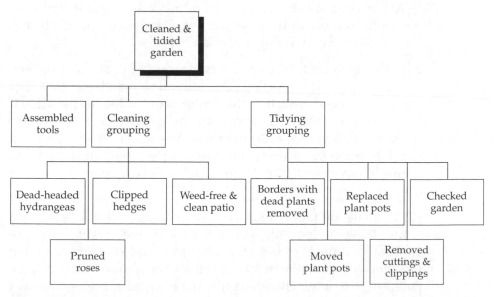

Figure 23 Work package for cleaning up the garden (product breakdown structure).

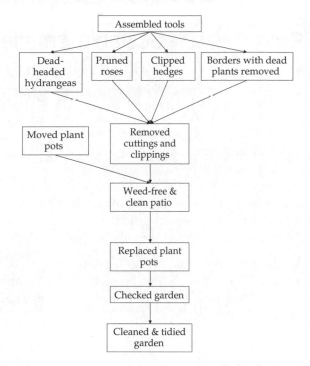

Figure 24 Product description for cleaning up the garden (product flow).

the work – you can imagine them checking against the product description and work package – before claiming that the final product has been delivered.

Figure 25 is an example of a form you might create for such jobs.

WORK PACKAGE							
Date of origin		Date allocated		Allocated to		Interface with	
Work package description							
Final product interfaces with							
Products to be produced							
Tools							
Effort		Cost		Start date		Target date	
Constraints							
Risks							
Reporting				Sign-off			

Figure 25 Example of a work package form for the cleaning up the garden job

2

Scalable smaller projects, or 'When you don't need a sledgehammer'

With some projects you get a 'gut feel' that 'the full glory' of PRINCE2 controls is not needed, but you are not certain what can be dropped and what should be retained in order to still have full control.

Introduction

The question is: 'Which elements of PRINCE2 can be relaxed or omitted on smaller projects?' There is no simple answer to this. Even small projects vary enormously in type and style.

Overall, the purpose of PRINCE2 can be regarded as reducing the risk of project failure. Thus, whenever any element of PRINCE2 is relaxed, this should be regarded as taking a risk.

What follows is a broad, structured approach to scaling down PRINCE2, based on key project characteristics. It begins by considering the *minimum* control elements necessary and, from that basis, builds in other control features of PRINCE2 as and when certain conditions prevail in a project.

The minimum PRINCE2 control elements for a small project

As a minimum, use the following checklist of elements of project management control on all projects, whatever the size and risks.

Organization

Every project should have:

- a project executive (or sponsor) – it must be clear who is authorizing work on the project
- a project manager – there should be clear understanding with all concerned as to who is responsible for the day-to-day management of the project.

If we consider the thoughts set out below, our organization structure of *actual people* might be as shown in Figure 26.

Often in small projects the executive can also be the senior user. Just ask yourself, 'who represents the users of the final product(s)?' – and remember, to be considered for a project board role, the person must have the authority to make the decisions required of that role.

What about the senior supplier role? Many people simply look at who is supplying anything to the project and assume that they must be a senior supplier. For example, take a project that will need some specialized paper for a document. Would it be sensible to put the stationery supplier on the board? Extremely unlikely. If you are the executive of a project to build a brick barbecue, would you put the builders' merchant on the project board? No, you would expect the project manager to simply go there and buy what the project wants. So in that case, how are you treating the senior supplier role? You have unconsciously decided to take on the role yourself. You have combined all three project board roles. If you think about it, this is how you have always treated small projects. It is common sense, and we keep saying that PRINCE2 is common sense.

If we move up to small projects within a company, it is often sensible to allocate the senior supplier role to the purchasing

Figure 26 Organization structure for a small project

manager, if the company has such a person. This is particularly useful in projects where we have a number of disparate suppliers who have no connection with each other. It would be foolish to give them all a part of the senior supplier role, and equally foolish to consider one of them representing the others. For example, if the project needs the hire of transport, the purchase of wood and the purchase of a computer, which single supplier would you select to represent them all? Does any one of them have any control over the others? Or would you give all three a part of the senior supplier role? It would be far more sensible to appoint either a person such as purchasing manager as senior supplier or combine the role with that of executive. This would take care of the authority needed to authorize expenditure on supplies, but it would leave the responsibility for supplier quality open. How would we tackle that?

Back to project assurance, the work package and the contract (or just your normal buyer's rights). In the product description in the work package you stipulate the required quality and define how the quality will be checked and who will do it. In most small projects the project staff who will use the purchased products will check that the goods are of the required quality but, if it needs to be done more formally or with special expertise, appoint someone to a (part-time?) project assurance role.

Remember that in many small projects, the project board members will be able to carry out their own project assurance. Get out the role descriptions in the PRINCE2 manual and discuss them with the person or persons who will be on the project board. Also remember that a role may be needed for only a short time. For example, the senior user role may need to delegate some project assurance activities to a business for only a short time in the project.

In a small project the project support role may often be taken by the project manager or shared between the team members. An example of this would be the configuration librarian's work. In a small project the work might take only a couple of hours a week.

Simple configuration management example

I recently visited a site working on a project for the Fleet Air Arm. They demonstrated a very simple configuration management method that reduced the configuration librarian's effort to about one hour a week. The project was a short one to produce a technical design study, and therefore did not have the complexity of having to handle many programmes or other products.

All configuration items had a prefix that indicated the contractor and the project. The letter M, T or Q to denote that the product was a management, technical or quality one followed this. Then another alpha character denoted the filing subsection and, finally, there was a sequence number to identify the document within the subsection. A filing log kept track of the sections, subsections and sequence numbers allocated.

All products that appeared in the project brief had a product description. These appeared in the one-stage plan and had the same unique reference. These products were kept to a fairly high level. For example, the project initiation document was one product. The stage plan showed each product broken down to sub-products, but these did not warrant a product description themselves. Each sub-product was broken down into the activities needed to create it.

All documents contained data in the page footer that included document title, configuration identifier, version number and date.

Each document had its own folder. In each folder there was an informal quality review log. Each product tended to go through several informal quality reviews. On completion of an informal quality review the owner of the product would advise the configuration librarian, and pass over a copy of the annotated product for safe-keeping in the folder. The librarian then updated the quality review (QR) log. The information kept about the review, and therefore about the product, was minimal, just the date and version number.

The version number was a two-part code. While the product was going through its initial creation the version was 0, and the sub-versions began at 'A' and ran through the alphabet. So, after three informal quality reviews a product would have the version '0.C'. Once the client had formally accepted the product, the version number became '1.0'. If that went back for change later, it would be renumbered '1.A', and so on.

The librarian kept a small summary of the status of each product. This was, in fact, only a copy from the informal QR logs of the latest known version level of each product and the date on which it was submitted to the library. The librarian would regularly take this to checkpoint meetings and get each team member to confirm that this was the latest status. If a product had moved on to a later version, the librarian would insist on the informal QR log being updated and on the relevant annotated product copies to be filed in the folder.

No other status information was kept. The version number was the only clue as to status.

This simple system meant that there was always a link between a product and its quality review(s). No action list was made out during these informal reviews; the product was just annotated with details of any changes required. Since a copy of the annotated product was filed away in the folder, the folders themselves formed the major quality file. In the project initiation document a section was defined as being the storage place for informal quality review results, but this was not used.

After the informal reviews there was always a formal review with the client, at which time a quality review action list was made out. There were separate sections of the quality file to hold invitation copies and results of formal quality reviews. For them, formal quality reviews were when the client attended, informal reviews were all those internal to the team.

They had created a document submission form, but had not found the need to use it, because they were only a small, localized team.

The librarian did not keep details of who had copies of a product, but felt that this was a function which would have to be added later in the project.

A project issue form had been designed but was very little used. The client had not come up with changes to the original brief, the team had not come up with any failures to meet the specification, and any minor questions had been dealt with by word of mouth. The project was only planned to take eight or nine weeks. I suspect that in a more typical project the need for formal use of project issues would have exposed the simplistic procedures that they had prepared.

Location information was held. This indicated the computer on which the text of the document was held in machine-readable format.

No formal details were kept of 'where used' data. At the foot of one of the documents there was space for the author to indicate usage, but this was little used. As the products were high-level ones and at an early stage in the life cycle of the final system, there were no sub-products, or at least the data kept did not go down to that level of detail.

Change control

You need some statement of how unexpected change will be controlled and a procedure to back this up.

Change control in a small project can be looked after by either the project manager or whoever has the configuration librarian role (see above). The more clearly the project brief/PID is/are defined, the less likely you are to need to use change control, but you must have it ready. Make it clear up front what the customer gets for the money and what procedure must be followed if the customer wants to change any requirement or specify a new requirement.

Business case

As PRINCE2 insists that there should be a business justification for every project, even a small project should have a form of business case. As a minimum the business case should give the reasons for the project and a summary of the options considered.

Does the project need to apply for funds? If the answer is, 'Yes', there will need to be some form of investment appraisal to show the project board what it will get for its money, and how long the return on the investment will take. If the answer is, 'No', then an investment appraisal is probably not needed. Before undertaking the creation of such an appraisal, ask if it is needed in order to get project approval – or, at least, authorization to enter initiation.

Will the expected benefits be checked after the project? If so, you will need to identify measurable benefits. If benefits will not be checked, you may be able to ignore that section of the business case.

Plans

As a minimum a PRINCE2 project needs a project plan. PRINCE2 also mandates a stage plan for every stage. If the project is small enough to be initiation plus one stage, can the project plan and the one stage be physically combined? Is the initiation stage so small that you can simply quote figures for it without doing a physical plan? For example, 'If I work on the PID with Fred, I could bring it in for approval on Wednesday'.

Do you need to break products down into activities? (i.e. do you need to do sub-process PL3?). Can you quite happily estimate resource and time needs from the product?

Can you plan by target date without a Gantt chart? If the project consists of a number of similar tasks, such as writing various chapters of a training manual or preparing a training course, if you have an idea of how long they should take on average, you can just make up a simple product checklist instead of creating a planning network and Gantt chart. That was how we wrote the PRINCE2 manual.

In a small project there will probably be no requirement for team plans.

Controls

Do you need highlight reports? If so, can they be oral rather than written? If the project has only one business stage, there will be no need for end stage assessments or end stage reports.

Can you combine the SU and IP processes, the project brief and the PID?

Risk

Even in a small project you need to consider the risks. But do you need a formal risk log, or are there so few risks that you can quickly run through all the risk documents?

Quality

You need to know to what level of quality the customer expects the product(s) to be built. Then you can identify what quality controls will be applied, by whom and to what. It would be dangerous to dive into a small project without this understanding. There may be no need for a formal project quality plan or stage quality plan, but, for example, the quality criteria should be defined in the product descriptions.

PRINCE2 documents

Project brief and project initiation document: you may choose to combine these, but whether you create one, both or have a programme supply the project brief, you need a statement – however 'brief' – of what the project is supposed to deliver.

You should create and agree with the project board a product description of the final product – and any other major products.

Filing

However simple, you need a project file including all relevant management and technical documentation.

Project closure

There must be some form of review of the final product with a deliberate sign-off and closure of the project.

These elements should be present in the management of every project.

A matrix approach

Patrick Mayfield and a large county council made a study of the project management needs of various sizes of project and came out with the following guidance.

The matrix can be a very useful guide to what level of PRINCE2 control is needed for a project that does not 'deserve' the full works. Figure 27 is the project control environment matrix. It suggests which other elements of control are relevant, given certain likely project conditions. For example, if you have a project with critical deadlines, then the use of a visual schedule, e.g. a formal Gantt chart, is really a 'must have'.

This is how the matrix works. First consider if a particular condition applies to your project. Some conditions are defined which may be required for your particular organization (for example, policy on project approval based on certain financial thresholds). Where a condition does apply, then follow the row to the 'Y', and then follow the column downwards to the lower half of Figure 27 labelled 'Control Elements Required'. Here you will find control elements that can supplement the minimum control environment.

On the matrix '✓' indicates that use of the control element is desirable on a project with this condition. A '☑' indicates that the control element is highly desirable. This means you could be inviting problems if you do not use it on your project.

The matrix is limited in its size because of considerations of the paper size used for the book. There are other items that ideally would appear on it. Let us have a look at a few of these.

Conditions/Features of Proposed Project													
Complex Dependencies?	Y												
Critical Deadlines?		Y											
Culture Change?			Y										
Duration up to 5 weeks?				Y									
Duration between 5 weeks and 3 months?					Y								
Duration greater than 3 months?						Y							
Effort greater than 180 days?							Y						
Management spread over two or more sites?								Y					
More than 2 User Teams?									Y				
More than 20 major end products?										Y			
Resource Intensive?											Y		
Estimated Spend > £5 000?												Y	
Estimated Spend > £50 000?													Y
Control Elements Required													
Business Case													
Statement of Benefits	✓	☑	☑	✓	✓	☑	✓		✓	☑	☑		
Full Business Case			✓			✓		✓	✓	✓		✓	☑
Organization													
Project Board			☑		✓	✓	✓	✓	✓	☑			☑
Delegation of Executive's Project Assurance role						✓		✓		✓		✓	☑
Delegation of Senior Supplier's Project Assurance role	✓	✓			✓	✓	✓			☑			✓
Delegation of Senior User's Project Assurance role		✓	☑					✓	✓	✓		✓	☑
Use of Team Manager(s)						✓				✓			
Planning													
Stage Plans, ESA's & Highlight Reports					✓	☑	✓		✓	☑			
Product Descriptions	☑	☑	☑	☑	☑	☑	☑	☑	☑	☑	☑	☑	☑
Product Breakdowns & Product Flows	☑	✓	✓	✓	✓	☑	☑			☑			☑
Network Analysis (Critical Path Analysis)	☑	✓								✓			
Gantt Charts	☑	☑	☑	✓	☑	☑	☑	✓	☑	☑	☑	✓	✓

Figure 27 Project control environment matrix

(continued)

Controls													
Statement of Tolerances	✓	☑	✓	✓	✓	✓	✓			✓			
Highlight Reports	✓	☑	✓	✓	☑	☑	☑	☑	☑	☑	✓	✓	✓
Use of Checkpoints		✓	✓		✓	✓	✓	✓	✓	✓		✓	✓
Full Project Change Control	☑	☑	✓		✓	☑	✓		✓	☑	✓	✓	☑
Risk Assessment Checklist		✓					✓	✓					☑
End Project Report	☑	☑	✓	✓	✓	☑	✓	✓	✓	☑	✓	☑	☑
Post-Project Review			✓		✓				✓	✓	✓	✓	✓
Lessons Learned Report	☑	☑	✓	✓	✓	☑	✓	✓	✓	☑	✓	☑	☑

Figure 27 (*continued*)

Team managers – the matrix only considers the elapsed time, but there are many other considerations, such as geographical spread of the development, any specialist skills required, the use of external suppliers.

Business case – the matrix only looks at projects costing either more than £5000 or more than £50 000. What about a small project costing less than £5000 – possibly only costing a few hundred pounds? For many small projects that are of the type 'one person wants a job doing, one other does the work' a business case may be nothing more than a reason for having the job done. I know that for many such projects my business case has been a balance of the cost of someone else doing it against how much I could earn doing my own job while they carry out the project. I call this the GALMI principle – 'get a little man in!' Another way of looking at it might be to compare the quality of an expert doing it compared to your amateurish efforts.

Let us consider an example. Suppose a characteristic of a project that emerges during the initial planning is that the total effort amounts to 245 days. Taking the condition labelled 'Effort greater than 180 days' we follow the row along to find the column with the appropriate controls. We find the following controls recommended as shown in Table 5.

In most projects, more than one condition will apply. How should two or more conditions on the matrix be combined? The rule is 'include all the elements suggested by any of the relevant conditions. If two conditions have different weightings of "Desirable", then choose the higher value'.

Table 5 Recommended controls.

Desirable	Highly desirable
Project board	Gantt charts
Stages, stage plans, ESA's	Product descriptions, product breakdowns, product flows
Statement of tolerance	Progress Gantt reports
Resource plans	Highlight reports
Statement of benefits	
Delegation of senior supplier's project assurance role	
Full project change control	
End project report	

Continuing the above example, supposing the condition 'Culture Change' was also found to apply. Combining the results of this condition with that of 'Effort greater than 180 days' would result in the recommended mix of control elements in Table 6.

Notice that with the new condition, some elements have been promoted to the 'Highly Desirable' status (e.g. project board), as well as some new ones being introduced (e.g. a full business case).

Note: The condition 'More than 20 major end products' means that more that twenty products are significant enough to be identified in the project plan, and progress will be reported on them to the project board.

Table 6 Recommended mix of control elements.

Desirable	Highly desirable
Stages, stage plans, ESA's	Project board
Statement of tolerance	Gantt charts
Resource plans	Product descriptions, product breakdowns, product flows
Full business case	Progress Gantt reports
Delegation of senior supplier's project assurance role	Highlight reports
Full project change control	Statement of benefits
End project report	User assurance
Post-project review	

The scaling matrix can become a part of organizational quality policy on which aspects of PRINCE2 and other elements of project management should be used on smaller projects. This means that an experienced project manager can be free to deviate from the recommendations of the matrix either by skipping recommended elements, adding some others, or both. If a manager does deviate from the matrix's recommendations then he or she must say so in the project quality plan section of the project initiation document, and justify why they are doing so.

At best the matrix is only a guide. Like so much in project management practice, it should not be followed slavishly but is just that – a guide.

Relaxing any PRINCE2 control element is taking a risk; do so with care.

4 A scaled-down project life cycle, or 'How to use big principles on small projects without becoming a sad bureaucrat'

This chapter proposes a complete package of a scaled-down version of the PRINCE2 method. It includes all the core minimum requirements for the method and is a version of the method that is worth inspecting to see if it meets the project management requirements of your environment. It is similar to the one designed and used very successfully by Tesco stores.

The project processes

A project has four processes:

- visualize
- plan
- do
- review.

Let us have a brief look at what steps are included in these processes.

Visualize

- Produce a basic draft project brief.
- Identify measures of success.
- Authorize the 'plan' process – yes or no.

Plan

- Appoint a project board and project team.
- Finalize the project brief and agree it with the project team and project board.
- Prepare detailed plans.
- Authorize the 'do' process – yes or no.

Do

- Action detailed plans.
- Manage and review project deliverables against plans.
- Track and report results.
- Agree any changes to targets.
- Authorize 'review' process – yes or no.

(There may be several iterations of the 'do' process if the project board and project manager decide to break the project into more than one stage.)

Review

- Hand over the finished products to the business unit.
- Review results and target changes.
- Review project performance.
- Authorize project completion – yes or no.
- Conduct post-project review.

The detailed steps

Visualize

Table 7

Step: Produce a project brief
Purpose: To clarify the details of the project

Key Activities	Considerations
Identify which business objective this project supports	Has a project brief already been produced? Who can contribute to the contents of the project brief?
Gather any background information, e.g. feasibility studies	What do you need to know to get the project started?

(continued)

Table 7 (*continued*).

Key Activities	Considerations
Write a product description of the final product	Is there common understanding of the final product?
Gather the necessary information to produce a draft project brief	What other documents are relevant?
Consult any relevant experts	On which teams will this project have an impact and at what point? Have all the support functions been considered?
Create a risk log	

Key Activities	Considerations
Design a project management team structure	Are business, user and supplier interests represented on the project board?
Confirm the structure and obtain commitment from those concerned	Is the representation – or communication need – of all stakeholders agreed?
Identify where ownership of the products will sit at the end of the project	Who can impact the start and performance of the project and handover of the product(s)? How will you agree ways of working with the project board and the team? Are any team-building techniques appropriate?

Key Activities	Considerations
Identify what impacts the project and products will have on the business	Have all impacts been identified?
Consult relevant measurement experts	Do any measurements need to be taken now in order to provide a baseline against which to measure the success of the delivered product?
Investigate areas where the impact is not clear	

Key Activities	Considerations
Agree the project brief with the executive, then the other members of the project board	How will the project brief be communicated and to whom? Who else needs to be aware of the project details?

(*continued*)

225

Table 7 (*continued*).

Key Activities	Considerations
Liaise with stakeholders. If authorized, proceed to 'plan' process	Who else needs to be involved in the project?
If not authorized, agree next steps	What do you need from the executive in order to begin the 'plan' process?

Table 8

Plan

Step: Plan the project
Purpose: To establish the management and resources needed to carry out the project

Key Activities	Considerations
Identify the project risks and countermeasures	Is any further detail required to clarify the project?
Agree what will be done and by whom	Do the measures of success fully reflect the impacts already defined? Do you need further information about the expected products in order to produce a plan? Are there any new or changed risks?
Plan the products, activities and timescales with the project team	What format of detailed plan is most appropriate for the team?
Produce a detailed plan	Does the 'do' plan contain enough time to do all the work, including quality inspection and assessment of any change requests?
Consult with the project team	What communication needs to take place, to whom and when?
Produce a communication plan as appropriate	What is the best way to keep the project board informed of progress? Is the standard highlight report content suitable for the project?
Agree the project plan with the project board	Does the project plan show that the required products can be produced within the time and budget constraints and to the required quality?
Agree tolerance levels with the project board	Is there any external data on what the project tolerances are?

(continued)

Table 8 (*continued*).

Key Activities	Considerations
If authorized, proceed to the 'do' process	
If not authorized, agree next steps	

Do

Table 9

Step: Action detailed plans
Purpose: To deliver the project's products and keep the project board and stakeholders aware of progress

Key Activities	Considerations
Allocate work to implement the detailed plans	Who is the most suitable resource to carry out a work package? Does the person or group agree the time required for a work package and have they the time? Has the work been evenly spread? Do the work commitments follow the plans dependencies and timetable?

Key Activities	Considerations
Monitor progress against the plans	How will intra-project team information be shared?
Monitor risks and update the risk log	What facts should be reported by the team in terms of progress?
Monitor the quality of the products being created/delivered	Are products being checked sufficiently against their quality requirements?
Produce highlight reports	Does the frequency and timing of reports need to be reviewed?

Key Activities	Considerations
Manage progress of the deliverables against the plan	Is it necessary to take corrective action to keep the project on track?
Record all proposed changes	Do plans and timescales need to be redefined?
Carry out impact analysis on proposed changes	Is the project still within the original scope identified?

(*continued*)

Table 9 (*continued*).

Key Activities	Considerations
Get agreement from the project board on the action to take about a change	Do agreed changes invalidate the current plan?
If authorized, proceed to 'review' stage	
If not, agree next steps	

Review

Table 10

Step: Handover to business
Purpose: To establish changes as part of day-to-day operations

Key Activities	Considerations
Confirm that the product is acceptable to the business	What are the plans for ensuring sustainability?
Agree handover process with the new owner	
Communicate change of ownership to the business	

Step: Review project performance
Purpose: To identify whether the project delivered successfully

Key Activities	Considerations
Review achievements against the project brief and plan	To whom does the review need to be communicated?
Review application of the project process	What form should the document take?
Review any use of business techniques	Can product success also be measured at this time?
Provide feedback to the team about their contribution	

(*continued*)

Table 10 (*continued*).

Step: Authorize 'project completion'
Purpose: To agree closure with the project board

Key Activities	Considerations
Consult with stakeholders Present the project review to the project board	
If completion not authorized, agree next steps	Do any next steps belong to the project team or the new owner?

Step: Conduct post-project review
Purpose: To assess the full business impact if outside the life of the project

Key Activities	Considerations
Complete the post-project review document	Are the measures of product success defined at the start of the project still valid? Does this review form part of the sustainability plans?

5 Chiselling away, or 'How much of this do I need?'

One way to tailor PRINCE2 for a small project is to match each process and component against the needs and environment of the specific project. There is no single right answer that will suit every project, but the following discussion should provide some pointers on how to tailor the method for your project. Let us start with the processes.

SU – starting up a project

There are some who want to tailor PRINCE2 for a small project whose first reaction is to say, 'We'll combine SU and IP'. You can see their thinking, 'Merge the creation of the project brief and the PID and go straight to DP2, "authorizing a project" '.

But there is more to SU than just the project brief. SU covers the design and appointment of the project management team. We need to preserve that in any merge of the two processes. The later discussion under the organization component covers the thought you need to have about who takes what role. The other products of SU can be produced in a merge of SU and IP; the customer's quality expectations, the project approach, the risk log and the project tolerances. You may do away with the initiation stage plan at the end of SU, but you will still need to plan what time and resources are needed for the combined SU and IP processes. Often with small projects we are talking of a small amount of time and resource, and you will be able to envisage this in a few minutes – that is, how much time you will need to 'plan' the combined processes, not necessarily how much time the two processes will take.

IP – initiating a project

The whole process is concerned with producing the one product, the PID. If you have combined it with SU, do not forget the SU products. Also do not forget that you need a project plan. You may feel that the rest of the project can be planned as one stage. If so, you have to decide if the detail of the single stage plan can be included physically in the project plan.

A major aim of initiation is to define precisely what is within the project's boundaries and – equally important – what is outside the scope of the project. This is just as important for a small project as for a large one. If you do not do this, it might be very difficult to close the project down when you have delivered what you believe to be the required products. There will always be other features, improvements that the user thinks of as the project progresses. A good project initiation document allows you to say, 'No, I'm sorry, but we didn't agree to do that'.

The other key part of the PID is the business case. Without a valid business case, you should not get past DP2. It may not be a full blown business case, but even for a small project there should be reasons, options and some idea of benefits.

The quality log and the issue log will also need to be created. If you are a 'regular' project manager, you probably have a daily log already. If not, now's the time to set one up.

DP – directing a project

Whether you need DP1 (authorizing initiation) will depend on what decisions you make about SU. If you combine it with IP, DP1 disappears. You do need DP2 (authorizing a project), however small the project. It may not take long, it may not be very formal, but there should be authority to move into the project based on a project plan and business case.

The need for DP3 (authorizing a stage or exception plan) partly depends on how many stages you have. If there is to be only one stage after initiation, that stage will be authorized as part of DP2. There is always the possibility, however, that even a small project might fall into exception and possibly cause the need for an exception plan. But that is not a bureaucratic overhead, just a necessary control. How formal or informal the exception assessment is a matter for the project manager to discuss with the project board.

I do not regard DP4 (giving ad hoc advice) as bureaucratic either. If the project is long enough to warrant highlight reports, presumably the project board will want to read them. If an exception situation arises, the project board will need to consider and make a decision, however brief a time this needs. There must also be a conduit for external information to be passed to the project manager. How much effort this takes is driven by the amount of external information that is relevant to the project. It may be nothing.

DP5 (confirming project closure) will still be needed. There is a saying that 'old projects never die, they just go on and on and on'. In other words, we have not been very good at closing projects. There are three parts to this: (1) at the beginning of a project we do not clearly draw the boundaries around what the project is to do; (2) we do not control changes to the requirements, and so the project becomes a rolling feast of additions and changes; (3) we lack the executive's control of the business case and budget. PRINCE2 gives us the chance to avoid all of these pitfalls, and the processes CP (closing a project) and DP5 provide the basis for a controlled close.

CS – controlling a stage

Even if our small project has only one development stage, we are going to use the CS process. It does not have to be very complex. Let us face it, it is simply:

- Allocate and agree work.
- Monitor that work until it is finished.
- Make any plan adjustments if they are required.
- Give progress reports to the project board if they have asked for them.
- Be ready to accept any project issues and deal with them.
- Discuss with the project board and resolve any exception situations.

Is there anything there that doesn't need to be done? I do not think so. In a small project much of this project management can be done informally. But please, please, write product descriptions and create work packages, at least for any other team members.

MP – managing project delivery

Will your small project have teams? Unlikely, so this process is combined with CS. MP1 (accepting a work package) will be combined with CS1 (authorizing a work package). MP2 (executing a work package) will be carried out – informally – by the team member to whom the work package is given, as will MP3 (delivering a work package). There should be no need for checkpoint reports unless some of the work packages take longer than, say, five to ten days. Confirmation that the work package has been completed should replace the need for further progress reporting.

SB – managing stage boundaries

Again we come back to the question of how many stages will your small project have. If you have only initiation plus one development stage, this process should not be needed – unless you have to prepare an exception plan, of course. If you have more than one development stage, you will need to use the full process for each stage after the first one.

CP – closing a project

You will need to close the project, however small. This is where you need to have written an unambiguous, complete project initiation document – especially the project definition and the acceptance criteria – and have a good working relationship with the executive. The last thing that you need with a small project is for it to drag on and on because of arguments on whether everything has been delivered. Let us have a look at the products of closure and see what work they might entail.

Project closure recommendation will at most be an informal word with the executive. Whether you need formal acceptance from the customer and those who will operate and maintain the final product depends on the environment and your relationships with those people. An informal word may suffice – ideally from them to the executive. Archiving the project records should be done, but is unlikely to require a major effort.

A check of whether there are any unfinished issues should be done (CP2). How much of a post-project review there will be has to be judged on the merits of each project, but it is likely that either no plan will be needed for it, or that only a simple plan is needed. For many small projects the benefits can be measured at the close of the project, thus not needing a plan.

A small project may or may not produce any lessons learned. Depending on the formality of the environment, it may be sufficient for the project manager to simply remember any lessons. If there are other project managers with whom information should be shared – and there are lessons that can be taken from the project – then a lessons learned report should be written. If no lessons were learned, do not write an unnecessary report!

Does the executive require an end project report? If so, must it be a formal document? For many small projects this can be done orally.

PL – planning

The size and complexity of the 'small' project will decide if the process needs to be done in detail. Start-up/initiation will probably be so small that it does not need to be formally planned. There probably will not be any team plans, so that leaves stage plans. How many will you have? We have already said that there is a good chance that there will be only one development stage. We may find it possible to insert the detail of this stage in the project plan. So you may be down to the need for one or two plans. Will you create a planning network and a Gantt chart for them or opt for the simpler product checklist? Will you need to draw product breakdown structures? You should have some process or technique that allows you to consider whether you have thought of everything, but the project definition will give you a good idea of how many products will be needed. But do still go through the thinking process. It is too easy to think, 'This is only a small project' and dash into it, only to find that you have forgotten a key product, whose absence causes a delay that takes you way beyond tolerances.

But, whatever else you do not do, start your small project by writing a product description for the final product.

Business case

Minimally you should be able to write down the reasons for doing the project. Have you genuinely considered alternatives, or whether the job should be done at all? Could you do it yourself? Do you need to hire an external supplier? Do you have the proven (and comparable) skills? Can you earn more money doing your own job than you will pay for an external supplier to do the 'project'? Have you compared it to the priorities of other jobs? Are you really certain that you know the probable costs of the work? Can it be afforded? Are you looking for financial benefits from the end product? Who holds the purse strings? Do they agree with you about the project?

Naturally every project, however small, should be a justifiable expenditure of effort. There are always more things clamouring for attention than there is money or resource available. So we need in some way to be sure that we are choosing the right project to do – and that the project will show some benefit in return for the effort. This does not mean that we have to carry out a full financial analysis for what we recognize as a small project.

Organization

It is unlikely that the full PRINCE2 project management structure will be needed. Wait a minute! If we remember our PRINCE2, we *will* need all the *roles*. It is just a case of what role combinations are sensible.

There are still people around who believe that you must have one person for each PRINCE2 project management team role, despite what the manual says. Consider the roles and ask yourself who has to make commitments – of money (executive), resources to do the job (senior supplier) and on behalf of those who will use the final product(s) (senior user). If the answer is the same person, then it is all right to have a project board of one person.

If it is a project (as opposed to a work package), there must be a provider of the funds, someone who is concerned with keeping the project in line with any higher level strategy. In other words, we need an executive.

Very often in small projects the executive can also take the senior user role. So who represents the supplier(s)? Let us take a closer look at this role.

The senior supplier is there to commit resources to develop the solution, ensure that any products supplied are of the required quality and resolve any supplier issues. If the project has suppliers who simply provide supplies off the shelf, e.g. stationery, hire tools, bricks, this does not mean that they should have part of the senior supplier role. How much of a commitment do you need from them? Would it be enough to have the customer's purchasing manager represent all such suppliers? Or would it be enough to combine the senior supplier role with that of executive? If it is genuine supplies that you need, as opposed to development staff, this may be enough.

Consider an example. A man owns a builders' merchant yard. One day he says to one of his men, 'I want you to take Fred and Jim and put up a large shed in that corner to protect this lot of material from the weather'. The owner will provide the money, he is stating the user's needs and he is supplying the labour. If the shed is to be bought from another supplier, that does not mean that the supplier has to take the position of senior supplier. The owner would handle that order himself or pass it to his purchasing manager. If the latter, maybe he takes part of the senior supplier role – the shed purchase, not the labour required – but does it need a special job description?

We will certainly need a project manager. The project manager is also likely to take on the team manager role.

Unless any detailed business knowledge is needed for the role, it is likely that 'the project board' will do its own project assurance.

Project support, including the role of configuration librarian, may be taken by the project manager or, better still, shared between the team members.

If in the example above the owner decided to be the project manager, do his own project assurance and project support, rather than make one of his people the project manager, you are moving towards the dividing line between a project and a work package. You would have to consider the other parts of the 'irreducible core' before making a decision on which to go for.

If your job needs more than one team, you have a project, not a work package.

Plan

Whatever the work, you need at least one physical plan. The minimum is a plan for the whole project – the project plan.

Could this plan go down to the level of detail required for day-to-day control without overwhelming the project board? ('Level of detail' means that the work is broken down into products or activities that each takes no more than, say, five days.) Would the amount of paper or number of screens needed to hold the detail be more difficult to understand than breaking it down into smaller stage plans? If the answer to the latter is 'yes', then you really do have a project. If your reaction is, 'no, I could put all the planning detail in one physical plan and still handle the work as a series of work packages', that is a small project. If the work can be contained at a detailed level in one plan and there is only one team involved, again you are moving towards a work package. If there is more than one team, you have a small project. Remember that if you use just one plan that satisfies both the overview (project plan) and detailed control needs (stage plan), in PRINCE2 terms you have had a project plan and one stage plan. You have simply combined them into one physical plan.

We have already touched upon the likely levels of plan that we will need – a project plan and plans for initiation and possibly only one development stage. We have already thought about physically combining these into one plan and whether we will need to draw product-based planning diagrams, a network plan and a Gantt chart. These may be beneficial. How complex is the project? If it is difficult to envisage the dependencies without putting it down on paper, then draw a product flow diagram. If you feel the need for a list of all the products that are required, start by drawing a product breakdown structure. By the way, if you draw mind maps, this is an excellent way to build a product breakdown structure.

Do we need to write a narrative for the plan? Have a think about what assumptions you are making. If you can see any danger or doubt about any of them, write them out. Have a think about the other contents of a plan narrative: approach, risks, interfaces, constraints. If you have to submit the plan to a 'real' project board for approval, it is best to write out a narrative – but briefly.

Control

Yes, we are going to need controls for even the smallest of projects – but possibly not all of them. As we discussed under the process 'managing stage boundaries', if we only have one development stage, we will not be using end stage assessments, so out goes the end stage report. If there is only one team, working directly under the project manager, we do not need checkpoint reports. The length of the project will indicate whether highlight reports are required. They may be, but probably only a few, and it is likely that the project board will only require a basic content, i.e. products finished in the reporting period, problems, products to be finished in the next period. You can probably get away without quality statistics, amount of budget spent and number of issues actioned. The project board may need a simple indication of progress against the target date, but any major news here would be dealt with in an exception report.

That brings us to tolerances. These should be used, however small the project. According to the individual project, you can discuss with the project board whether tolerances are required for all six tolerance types: cost, time, quality, scope, benefit and risk. It may be possible to drop some of these.

We will need some form of project initiation document. Again a review of each of the headings will tell you whether you need to use them all. But be careful; if you miss out a heading, might the customer/user use this as a lever, saying that something that you have not done was implicit? Look at the environment and decide how well you need to 'watch your backside'.

Is the work so risky that there should be several key events when decisions on whether to continue or not should be made? If so, that means the use of stages, and that means that you have a small project. It is easy to compare the PRINCE2 controls for a project against those for a work package and decide where your job falls.

Risk

Beware of using this as a sign of whether you have a project or not! Sometimes a piece of work will be so trivial that we might be tempted to believe that we do not need to consider risk. If you have reached adulthood, you will have sufficient painful memories of failing to consider risks that we really do not need to discuss this topic any more. All work needs a method of thinking about and handling risk.

You really need to follow the whole risk procedure through. Documentation may be quite informal, but do remember the phrase, 'Project management is risk management. All the rest is administration'. If you have a serious effort at risk analysis when creating the project plan, this should cover most of your needs. Put in monitoring 'events' in your daily log, and you should be doing as much as you need to on risk.

Quality

Is quality a consideration? Might there be a difference between the level of quality required and the level of quality provided? Are there various standards that must be met (legal, legislative or demanded by the customer)? Will there be an external quality assurance department that needs to inspect the products and the ways in which quality is built into them? Whatever the work is, quality will be a consideration. The more quality needs to be planned, the more independent quality checkers there are, and the more likely it is that you have a project.

If you write out a product description for the final product at the outset, this should suffice as the customer's quality expectations. If they are measurable, they should also do as a big part of any acceptance criteria; possibly needing only time and cost criteria to be added.

Check carefully with the customer and users whether there are standards to be met. Nothing is worse than blasting through a small project, only to find that you have not conformed to a standard that 'they would have told you about, if only you'd asked'.

The type of quality checks that will be needed depend on the type of products that you have to deliver. My suggestion would be that if there is a product that takes a lot of the whole project time to deliver, find some way of checking its quality as it is being built. Do not wait until it is built. Correction of errors can take as much time as the original build. Do remember that the vast majority of errors found in products stem from poor specification, and secondly poor design. Do not wait until the build to inspect it.

Configuration management

You know the rule; if the product that you develop has more than one version, more than a few components or more than one person working on it, you are doing configuration management. So, judged against this, do you need it? If you do, you can probably share the configuration librarian's job between the team members – or do it yourself. A very simple identification scheme will probably be enough; a name for each product and a version number. Please do not overwrite a document with changes; create a new version and change that. You never know when you will need to go back to answer some question or retrieve something from an old version.

Project issue management

Be ready for project issues. You may not get any, but at least have the blank form ready and know what procedure to follow if any issues arise. As with larger projects, the person doing configuration management should also take this job on.

Product-based planning

We discussed under plans whether you needed to use this technique. We said at that time that it was essential to write at least a product description for the final product. Whether you need to write other product descriptions depends on the project. If you cannot immediately envisage what you would write for a product under the product description headings, then you probably need to write one out.

Many small projects will not require diagrams, but if you have ten or more products and integration products, it is worth drawing a product flow diagram as a basis for checking the sequence of doing things. This need only be a rough drawing on a piece of paper, but it does help the thinking process.

Quality review

If there are documentation products (business products rather than PRINCE2 management products), then it is sensible to quality review them. Remember, an informal review can be held between two people.

Change control

Again, every job needs a method of change control – unless you do not care what it costs, how long it takes or what the finished product looks like or how it performs. If this is the case, then you are still using change control. You have just put it in the hands of the supplier, and the supplier's measures and business case may differ from yours (e.g. is there more money in it for the supplier to make changes?). So you need change control whether it is a project or not. If the answer to the question, 'Who needs to approve changes?' is someone higher than the project manager, then it looks as if you have an executive and/ or senior user, and therefore a project.

In a small project there should not be many requests for change, but you need to have a procedure and a form ready. The better you do the project definition in the first place, the less likely you are to have to handle change requests. Make sure at the outset that the project board understands that there will be extra costs and time associated with changes.

Managing projects at GCHQ

Government Communications Headquarters are users of PRINCE2. They came across the problems of matrix management and have found a way to resolve the project resourcing problems that this can cause. This description of their approach is included in this book because the concepts that surround the implementation of minor projects and the use of work packages triggered off the earlier chapter in this book on their use in very small projects. The approach is worth reading on its own merits to avoid projects being top heavy with resources that cannot be used all the time.

Improvement programme

A programme is under way at GCHQ that addresses people, process and tools in a co-ordinated manner. Its scope includes: the migration to OGC's recommended practice for programme management; the adoption of PRINCE2; the training and 'professionalization' of project managers; and preparation for an integrated management information system (MIS). It also includes the implementation of some unique concepts, which are enabling the matrix organization to work more effectively and efficiently in delivering projects and technical services.

Matrix management

Government Communications Headquarters has a project and technical engineering group modelled on the classical matrix organization (Figure 28). The technical engineering group employs over 1000 staff in fourteen functional areas. Each area specializes in a technical field, e.g. networking and communications,

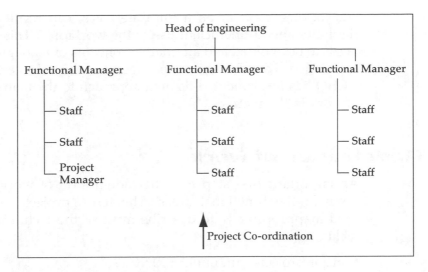

Figure 28 Balanced matrix

desktop systems, etc. Staff are engaged on over 200 projects in addition to delivering a range of services. Projects often span more than one functional area. Government Communications Head-quarters has suffered from over-committing the functional areas, leading to conflicts in priorities and work delays, with consequential impacts on project schedules.

The need for a matrix

As with many other organizations with a large number of projects, there is a tendency for people to be involved in more than one project at the same time, as well as retaining responsibilities for background work. While a matrix organization is commonly used in these situations, its application in GCHQ has resulted in a considerable planning and scheduling challenge for the functional managers who have to balance the competing demands on their workforce.

The functional groups are the work engine behind the project system and if these resources are not managed effectively the project managers will be unable to bring in their projects on time and to budget. The alternative practice to matrix management, i.e. assigning large numbers of people to project teams and locking them in on a full-time basis, can result in poor flexibility and an inefficient use of the workforce. This practice needs to be avoided and alternative concepts of managing work are needed. To tackle these weaknesses of the balanced matrix, GCHQ has implemented its own approach to the management of work in the matrix.

Redefinition of work

An important first step was the redefinition of work undertaken in the functional areas. The term 'project' had been used inappropriately to describe most of the technical work, including:

- major projects, run under PRINCE2
- minor projects, run under GCHQ minor project procedures
- background work, such as technical support.

It was necessary to redefine what was meant by a project, and to introduce additional terms to reflect the different nature of the other types of work. This is illustrated in Figure 29.

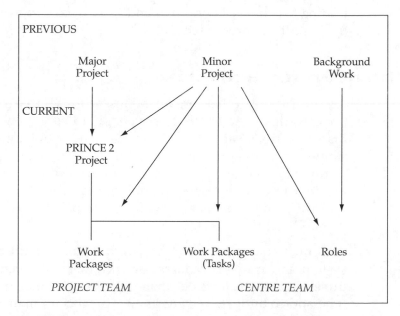

Figure 29 Redefinition of work

PRINCE2 projects

Government Communications Headquarters has been a user of PRINCE since 1991, and has benefited from this consistent approach to managing its major projects. The recent introduction of PRINCE2, and OGC's latest guidance on programme management, provided an opportunity to reconsider the way programmes and projects are managed. Under the new definitions, the term 'project' is only used to refer to work that can be managed as a PRINCE2 project. This is largely the work that would previously have been a major project. All projects and associated technical work now form parts of a small set of strategic programmes.

Work packages

Some work that would previously have been considered a minor project may continue to be a project run under PRINCE2 if its importance and independence makes this desirable. Consequently, there continue to be a few small projects, but most of the minor projects are being more accurately defined as PRINCE2 work packages within another project. This allows all related work to be managed under a single project, rather than as several related small projects. This dramatically reduces the number of projects, the project management overheads, puts responsibility for project management with one project manager, and allows technical business to focus on product delivery.

Project teams

The term 'core project team' is used to refer to the people who have been formally assigned to work on a project, for a specified proportion of their time over a calendar period. While working on the project they report to the project manager, not their line manager. The concept of a core project team allows more formal agreement on who is going to work on a project and when, and gives direct control to the project manager. Responsibility for work packages undertaken by the core project team rests with the project manager, although this may be delegated to a team manager, within the project team.

Centres

In many cases it may not be a practical or efficient use of resources to assign people to a project team, as these people may be working on several projects and may have other background work to do. Instead, they are managed as a number of groups called centres. A functional manager may be responsible for one or more centres in his or her area, each of which will be managed by a centre manager. The project manager can agree to place work packages, along with authorized funding, with these centres. The centre manager takes responsibility for who works on a work package and the scheduling of this work in order to deliver the products to the agreed quality and completion date. This is very similar to 'contracting out' a piece of work to an external supplier. The centre manager is thus operating as a PRINCE2 team manager.

Roles

Work that is not directly associated with any one project, and typically needs to be done throughout the year, is undertaken as a role. Examples of role work include liaison, internal consultancy and technical support. Everyday management and staff activities (such as training, leave and sickness) are not defined as roles, so as to retain the distinction between these overhead activities and background work. Roles are mostly of a technical nature, but would also include non-technical activities such as clerical support. People within a centre will work both on work packages and in roles. For example, the people working on a work package may also be responsible for supporting the products in a previous work package, as part of an appropriate support role.

Centre management

A centre manager agrees to undertake roles throughout the year, at the same time as agreeing appropriate resources with a sponsor. He or she will agree to undertake work packages for project managers on a one-by-one basis, agreeing the details for the work and timescale, based on the centre's capability and current workload. Alternatively, the centre manager can assign staff to project teams for set periods. The centre manager will plan the centre's work, on a day-to-day basis, making use of the people in the most efficient and effective way to deliver against the role, work package and project assignment obligations.

Project management

The concept of centres presents a choice for how the project work will be done. Staff can be assigned to the project team, and work under the direct control of the project manager. Alternatively, work can be put out to a centre with an agreed work package acting as the 'contract'. A combination of the two mechanisms may be used. For example, in a project to deliver a new IT system the application software could be written by the project team, but deployment to desktops could be done by the desktop centre, as a work package. In due course, the desktop centre may provide ongoing support for the desktop component within one of its support roles.

Resource allocation

Centres may contain a few people, or over fifty. A centre may have a number of roles and work packages in its current workload. It may also have some people assigned to projects, on a full- or part-time basis. The manager of a centre needs some way of recording the people in the centre, the activities, and the commitments that the people have to these activities. When being asked to accept a new work package, it is important that the existing commitments are understood, in terms of how much time will be needed on each activity, so that appropriate timescales can be agreed for the new work package.

When planning the work for the centre, there are two considerations: first, that the roles, work packages and project assignments should be executed as agreed and, secondly, that everyone in the centre should be used as effectively and efficiently as possible. There are many project management tools and techniques to assist the project management function but few to assist the centre manager with resource allocation.

A resource allocation database has been created to help in this area. It records the people, activities and commitments people have against the activities over a twelve-month calendar period. From this it is possible to produce outlooks by person or activity, showing the forward work plan. Using time sheets, the time spent on activities is fed into the same database, so that actuals can be compared with forecasts. A monthly baseline is taken, so that this information can be compared month by month.

Benefits

Although the improvement programme is still under way, and work continues on developing the longer term MIS, a number of benefits are already evident:

- Centres help establish core teams with business knowledge and skills that can be effectively and efficiently used across a number of projects, as well as being available for support if needed.
- The people in a centre benefit from being part of a permanent team, able to share ideas and problems with colleagues. They can take ownership for work that has been better defined and have a better understanding of what is required of them and by when.
- Identification of core project teams helps clarify exactly who is working on the project and when. This helps both the project and centre managers plan their resources, and improve the accuracy of their timescale estimates.
- The rationalization of projects into fewer 'real' projects is simplifying the introduction of PRINCE2. It is also helping to clarify the position of the project manager and to distinguish project management from technical management. This also gives staff a better understanding of project, technical and line management duties, when planning their careers.
- The identification of roles helps the understanding and quantification of background work. This allows better decisions to be made concerning priority, the budget and resources it should receive.
- The resource allocation database provides an improved understanding of current workloads and trends. It has also led to more accurate estimates and provides improved information for resourcing decisions.

- A customer/supplier relationship has been created between projects and centres, both in terms of the execution of work packages and the supply of people to work in project teams. This has encouraged a clearer division of responsibilities, and has provided a clean separation between project and line management.

In conclusion

The work detailed here is already providing evidence of success. In one pilot area, the increase in work throughput with the same resources has been estimated at 30 per cent. Although more modest improvements are expected overall, even a 3 per cent improvement in the use of resources would represent thirty additional staff, or an efficiency gain on the salary bill of over £1 million per annum. Government Communications Headquarters can look forward to delivering increased value for money to its customers in a way that not only maximizes the effectiveness and efficiency of its programme and project resources, but also enhances flexibility and dependability in the use of these resources.

Summary

In this book, we have seen six possible approaches to the management of small projects under PRINCE2:

- Use the principle of work packages to handle small one-off 'projects'.
- Use the minimum elements necessary for control.
- Select the aspects of PRINCE2 that you should use according to a 'sizing' matrix.
- Produce an abbreviated version of PRINCE2 that keeps the essentials.
- Consider how much of each part of PRINCE2 is required for a specific project.
- The GCHQ method of handling staff allocation.

Which one is right for your project? Only you can tell. According to the different projects you tackle, you may need more than one of these approaches. For the small stand-alone tasks or 'projects' I would recommend the work package approach. For larger projects, I would use the scaling matrix.

We really have to consider the irreducible core of PRINCE2:

1. When deciding whether we have a genuine project.
2. Deciding what elements of the method we need to use.

So, what is the irreducible core of PRINCE2?

Irreducible core of PRINCE2

Please, please, remember that if there was to be only one element of PRINCE2 that you use, make it the product description.

If you find reasons for discarding everything else, this really is the one item that you must have. As soon as you are presented with a job, whatever its size, sit down and write a product description of the final product. You will find out so much about the job to be done, the skills needed, what inputs you need, and it starts you off immediately thinking about quality.

However, there are other parts of PRINCE2 that can play a vital part.

If you have a project, it will need:

- a business case
- a project organization (even if it's only identifying who is responsible for what)
- one or more plans
- a method of handling risks
- a method of change control
- definition of the quality expectations and a recognition of how that quality will be built into the products and how this will be tested
- a series of controls that match the organization and the size of the project.

Do not forget that if there is more than one person working on the project, or more than one version of any product, you will also need some level of configuration management.

Remember that PRINCE2 recommends, nay, begs, you to scale these elements in relation to the size and complexity of the project. Just because the work that you have to undertake matches up with the above 'irreducible core', suggesting that it needs to be treated as a genuine project, this does not mean that you need a battalion of people, an armful of documents and a rigid structure of controls that force you to write reports every few hours. Have a look at each of them and use common sense as to how much is needed. As the PRINCE2 manual says, 'how much do I need in order to have the project under control?' If your decision is to ignore one or more completely without consideration, do not complain if the element that you have ignored jumps up and bites you before you have finished.

Last thoughts

The sizing matrix approach gives you more flexibility than the 'abbreviated' version approach in deciding how many of the PRINCE2 processes and components to use. With the abbreviated version, you might still be using too much 'bureaucracy'. The work package is a good discipline for really small 'projects' that do not need some of the elements discussed above. The guidelines should indicate to you whether your job could be handled as a work package or as a small project.

Remember, PRINCE2 is so flexible and scalable that it does not introduce unneeded bureaucracy. If something needs doing, it needs doing. By all means adjust the scale or formality of doing it, but do not just drop it.

Index

Page numbers in **bold type** refer to figures; those in *italic* to tables